Sticks and Stones

Sticks and Stones

Karen L. Maudlin, Psy.D.

W Publishing Group™

www.wpublishinggroup.com

A Division of Thomas Nelson, Inc.
www.ThomasNelson.com

STICKS AND STONES
by Karen L. Maudlin

Copyright © 2002 Karen L. Maudlin.
Published by The W Publishing Group,
a Division of Thomas Nelson, Inc.,
P.O. Box 141000, Nashville, Tennessee 37214.

Produced with the assistance of The Livingstone Corporation.
Editorial work by Joan Guest and Paige Drygas;
additional concept help and stories from April Carlson.

ISBN 0-8499-4356-6

Printed in the United States of America

02 03 04 05 06 07 PHX 9 8 7 6 5 4 3 2 1

Dedication

For *Katie and Alexa*, my most precious gifts from God.

Thank you for continuing to teach me that respect
is a two-way street that needs to be traveled on a daily basis.

For *Ben and Anne Grimshaw*, my grandparents,
who make my world a safer place.

Contents

Acknowledgments

I want to thank my family for their love, encouragement, and patience (did I mention patience?) during this project. For my girls, thank you for the maturity of understanding the time and energy away and your ability to understand that "almost done" really does precede "done." I want to thank my sister, Nancy, for her steadfast encouragement in my life. You have always urged me to follow my dreams and to stand up for myself. Your guidance as an older sister helped me learn how to deal with bullies early in life.

It is hard to describe all my appreciation for the fine editorial hand of the best editor I know, my husband Mickey. I am grateful for your tireless wee morning hours of editing, refining, and shaping this book.

Thanks to my editors at The Livingstone Corporation, Paige Drygas and Joan Guest, for their contribution to the project. It was Livingstone's vision for this book that made it happen.

I want to thank all the school administrators for sharing so freely your wealth of knowledge and experience. I admire your passion to educate kids both in their minds and in their character. I appreciate all the parents for sharing your stories from the school of hard knocks in dealing with bullying in your children's lives.

I especially want to thank all the children and adolescents who shared their painful stories and their courageous lessons in order to help other kids and adults learn and grow in their respectfulness toward others.

Chapter One
What Is Bullying?

Character is a diamond
that scratches every other stone.

—Cyrus A. Barton

Hamad's[1] family moved to North America after living amid violence in the Middle East. Hamad's father was happy with the life they had found. "We came thousands of miles . . . away from war . . . to a country that is safe and peaceful." But Hamad, a fourteen-year-old high school student, was not happy. What he didn't tell his parents or younger brother was that school had become "horrible, horrible." Kids called him names—"gay, queer, fag." One student punched him in the stomach. In March 2000, Hamad wrote, "I tried to cope with it but I couldn't take it anymore." After leaving a seven-page letter to his parents absolving them of guilt, he took a walk. He filled his backpack with rocks, made his way to the bridge between New Westminster and Surrey, B.C., and jumped to his death. His parents' most haunting thought is that he never told them of his troubles.

Hamad was a victim of bullying. While suicide is an

extreme response to bullying, the wounds from verbal and physical harassment run deep. Carol, a college junior, can remember vividly the day in fifth grade when a group of boys started to call her "Shamu," after the killer whale at Sea World. For many children, bullying is their first encounter with evil. They come face to face with forces that are not just neutral toward them but are actively malicious. Thus bullying can have a profound, life-shaping effect on its victims.

According to a recent study published in the *Journal of the American Medical Association*, nearly 30 percent of children report being involved in bullying, either as a bully or as a victim, in the past year—10 percent as victims, 13 percent as bullies, and 6 percent as both bully and victim. A staggering 8 percent said they were bullied at least once weekly.[2] The report also confirmed what many other studies have found: Bullying is most common in the middle school, or junior high, years and decreases as kids enter the later teenage years.

While 30 percent of kids report being involved with bullying in the last year, when researchers asked how many have *ever* been involved with bullying, either as a bully or as a victim or both, the percentage rises dramatically. One study of students from the Midwest found that over the course of their middle and high school careers, "76.8 percent of students . . . say they have been bullied and 14 percent of those students indicated that they experienced severe reactions to the abuse."[3] Because so many kids are affected, parents, teachers, administrators, and youth workers need to be alert. (See Appendix B for myths and facts.)

Yet there is a strange silence about a problem that affects so many families. Few schools actively work to educate parents and students about bullying. And for parents, bullying is an easy problem to want to minimize or write off as "boys being boys" or "girls being catty." Often we simply do not face and confront the problem.

Our culture tends to inoculate us against the impact of small violent and disrespectful actions, treating them as rites of passage for our children. But another statistic reveals the lie behind that attitude. One study found that "60 percent of those characterized as bullies in grades 6–9 had at least one criminal conviction by age 24."[4] In fact, research shows that school bullies become adult bullies, using their primitive tactics to get their way in adult life. In other words, if students and schools don't intervene to show bullies that their behavior is unacceptable, society will have to teach them a much harder lesson later in life, probably after many more people have been victimized.

THE DENIAL FACTOR

The reason we underplay the problem is that the issue of child safety makes us as parents uneasy. We are uncomfortable with the thought that our children will confront evil without our protection. So it is hard to face problems that we know are complicated or that we feel we have no control over.

Take courage. It is only in facing the problem that we will be able to challenge and reduce it in our schools and communities. In fact, the single most effective factor in reducing bullying is adult intervention.

The National School Safety Center estimates that over half a million "attacks, shakedowns, and robberies" occur in an average month in public secondary schools. And, according to one estimate by the National Education Association, as many as 160,000 students miss school every day because they fear attack. Dealing with bullies is not an uncommon problem facing our children.

Our schools are not the places they once were. Schools today are more overcrowded, potentially lethal (with drugs and weapons available), and racially and ethnically diverse, which adds complexity and tension to the school atmosphere. Basic respect for authority can no longer be assumed. Stories of teachers being threatened, hit, or even shot appear in our newspapers every year.

If you think it is someone else's school where bullying occurs, think again. "While direct physical assault seems to decrease with age, verbal abuse appears to remain constant. School size, racial composition, and school setting (rural, suburban, or urban) do not seem to be distinguishing factors in predicting the occurrence of bullying."[5]

Preparing kids in elementary school with assertiveness skills, knowledge, and self-confidence for the junior high onslaught is essential. Establishing effective bully intervention strategies with parents, teachers, and students can dramatically affect the entire emotional experience of school for many students.

KIDS ARE PEOPLE, TOO

In the twenty-first century, many say civility is dead. From road rage to simple rudeness, from the Columbine shootings to the World Trade Center attack, showing respect to one another is an increasingly rare virtue. But it is a necessary virtue for society to work.

In churches and schools, we often hold up the intrinsic values that children are gifts from God (in the church) and that they are worthy of respect and dignity (in the schools). However, we often fall short of living out those values. Do we really hold the same standards for respect for children as we do for adults?

A seven-year-old boy is bathing at night and his mom notices bruises on his arm. "What happened to you?" asks the mom. The boy begins to cry as he reluctantly admits that a known bully waits for him on the playground each day and hits him if he doesn't let him cut in line for tetherball. The mom suggests the boy stop playing tetherball and avoid the bully, and reminds him that soon he'll be older and won't have to deal with this anymore.

That sounds like wise counsel. But imagine that the woman's husband comes home from work and says that yet again his colleague punched him at the office. Would she suggest that her husband avoid the department where the bully works? Would she assure him that someday he will be the boss and then not have to worry about the bully?

No. No adult should have to tolerate being physically harmed at work. Why is the same scurrilous behavior relegated to a less important status if it occurs with children? If behavior is abusive when it occurs to adults, then it is also abusive if it occurs with children. Unintentionally we are conveying a double standard for our children.

What is respect anyway? According to Louise Dietzel, school counselor and Head Start consultant, "Respect is a process of regarding, valuing, considering, recognizing, and appreciating. It is being genuine, kind, courteous, open, honest, fair, equitable, tolerant, and consistent."[6] She goes on to describe respect as the basic psychological need to be "recognized, esteemed, appreciated, valued, listened to, and heard."[7] Another way of saying this is the Christian Golden Rule: Treat others as you would want to be treated.

Respect, like self-esteem, is learned, and the two values are interdependent. Self-esteem is loving oneself in a way that includes "self-acceptance, self-respect, self-monitoring, and a willingness to forgive yourself when you make a mistake, even simple obvious ones."[8] True self-esteem also involves empathy for others. As the old adage goes, "I'm okay, you're okay," not, "I'm great, you stink." Empathy is the key ingredient missing from every bully's repertoire. Cockiness and self-confidence are two qualitatively different characteristics, even though they may look similar on first blush. Are we, as parents, loving ourselves and modeling respect for our children?

When respect is absent, the law of the jungle takes over. And a common behavior in such an environment is bullying.

TYPES OF BULLYING

After the season of school shootings, the spotlight is on schools, and parents of school-aged children and teachers are frantic to find ways to equip their children and protect them from harm at school. The key characteristic identified in every known case of lethal school violence is bullying. Either the perpetrators were bullies or the victims of others' bullying. After much study and research, many experts recommend creating a zero tolerance environment for bullying as the critical key for making our schools and neighborhoods safe for our children. (Later we will explore what "zero tolerance" should mean. Many educators suggest that they retain some flexibility in what they administer as a consequence for bullying.)

This book is a handy guide for parents, teachers, school administrators, and youth workers (coaches, pastors, community workers, etc.) to institute intervention and prevention programs with preteens and teens. Our first task is to understand what bullying is and then to observe how it affects victims, bystanders, and bullies themselves. Only then can we proceed to what we can do to prevent and handle bullying.

This complex problem needs coordinated efforts from parents, teachers, and students alike. Accordingly, tools for both adults and children are provided. The central concept of the book is *respect*. Teaching, modeling, practicing, and instilling respect at every level of interaction is the best tool against bullying. Respect is the key ingredient if we want to empower kids to have self-esteem, to display courage in the face of intimidation, and to show compassion for the underdog. Teaching kids to respect themselves and others is the best antidote for neutralizing potentially threatening situations.

Summarizing the latest research, Ron Banks describes the range of behaviors encompassed by the term bullying. "Bullying is comprised of direct behaviors such as teasing, taunting, threatening, hitting, and stealing that are initiated by one or more students against a victim. In addition to direct attacks, bullying may also be more indirect by causing a student to be socially isolated through intentional exclusion. Whether the bullying is direct or indirect, the key component of bullying is that the physical or psychological intimidation occurs repeatedly over time to create an ongoing pattern of harassment and abuse."[9]

Bullying always involves abuse. But how can a parent make the distinction between normal childhood teasing and actual bullying? Bullying experts Suellen and Paula Fried identify six characteristics that distinguish normal childhood badgering from bullying.

1. *Intent to Harm*—the perpetrator finds pleasure in the taunting and continues even when the victim's distress is obvious.
2. *Intensity and Duration*—the teasing continues over a long period of time and the degree of taunting is damaging to the victim.
3. *Power of the Abuser*—the abuser maintains power because of age, strength, size, and/or gender.

4. *Vulnerability of the Victim*—the victim is more sensitive to teasing, cannot adequately defend himself or herself, and has physical or psychological qualities that make him or her more prone to vulnerability.

5. *Lack of Support*—the victim feels isolated and exposed. Often, the victim is afraid to report the abuse for fear of retaliation.

6. *Consequences*—the damage to self-concept is long lasting, and the impact on the victim leads to behavior marked by either withdrawal or aggression.[10]

All children will confront teasing and taunting from their peers. Having your children come home in tears because their classmates said or did something mean is to be expected. Having your children come home bruised and afraid to go to school is not. Nor is it normal to have your children come home every day in tears.

While the stereotype of bullying is physical harm, it can encompass a wide set of other behaviors, including verbal, emotional, and sexual abuse.

Verbal abuse can vary dramatically from simple but intense name-calling, badgering, and harassment to sophisticated brainwashing techniques. Boys tend to be into simple name-calling, whereas girls, often more verbally sophisticated than boys at the preteen age, can launch complicated smear campaigns that ruin the victim's reputation. Verbal abuse can also include threatening to spread rumors or embarrassing information or "dissing" the student in front of peers.

Susan was verbally and emotionally bullied by a popular group she desperately wanted to be a part of. On one occasion, she was invited to a sleepover only to arrive and be told in front of the other girls that she was not welcome.

Emotional abuse can take the form of black-balling a child

from parties, groups making a pact to ostracize a child from being picked at gym, or ignoring a student whenever they are together. The ongoing nature of the mistreatment causes the child to believe there must be something wrong with him or her.

Lauren had played on the same softball team with the girls from her school since kindergarten, but in fourth grade she moved across town. Her parents didn't want her to lose all those friendships, so they made sure she continued to play on the same softball team. Despite her parents' commitment to driving her across town a few times a week, Lauren painfully discovered that she was on the outside with these girls. No one talked to her. No one greeted her when she arrived for practice or a game. The coach was welcoming and friendly, but the girls made her pay for moving. Lauren continued to have individual teammates over to play, which always went well. But then no one invited her over. She felt even more devastated when a girl who was friendly one day in private would snub her the next when in a group. Lauren became convinced that something was wrong with her since no one wanted to be her friend. She even became convinced that she was bad at softball. Lauren's parents eventually decided to put Lauren on another softball team that had girls from a variety of schools.

A common result of emotional abuse is intense humiliation. An example is the group that grabbed a thirteen-year-old boy in the locker room showers and carried him outside, leaving him there naked in front of girl students. While parents and teachers in the past may have considered this "boys being boys," the damage this type of incident leads to is far from normal. Intense humiliation generated from the attack fans the fire of retaliatory acts that may lead to school violence but always lead to damaged self-esteem of the victim and frequently the bystanders as well.

An often overlooked component of bullying is negative peer pressure to do something dangerous, usually with the vague promise that the victim will be more "included" as a result. Kids can dare or coerce others to try drugs by ridiculing them as cowards if they refuse. An extreme example, common in gangs, is challenging a boy to demonstrate his value and loyalty by beating up or even murdering a rival gang member or bystander.

In his book *Best Friends, Worst Enemies: Understanding the Social Lives of Children*, author Michael Thompson tells the tragic story of one of his nephew's friends named Patrick. Patrick was a popular high school sophomore. He and twenty-five other students went to a remote area by a river. There a bridge crossed the river. It had become the location of a traditional challenge where brave boys jumped from the bridge into the river. Patrick said he would do it. But when he climbed up to the spot where people usually jumped, he kept climbing. That's when the others started to egg him on. At one point Patrick said he was too high and started to back down, but they all teased him and urged him to continue. He did. Jumping from a height of sixty feet into eleven feet of water, he never surfaced.[11] We need to teach kids to listen to their internal judgment foremost and disregard peer pressure that is careless and idiotic.

In some fraternities, date rape is a way to establish oneself as a full member. Parties are organized to facilitate such activity without detection. Date rape in high school is becoming more common. On the preteen level, the "dare" might be to grab a girl's breast in the hallway at school.

Since the most significant bullying behaviors correspond to the time when kids are beginning to go through puberty, it should be no surprise that sexual harassment is a common type of bullying. Again we need to distinguish between mere missteps during a confusing developmental stage and what is truly abusive. The Task Force on Juvenile Sexual Offending puts these qualifications on what should be considered *sexual abuse*: "sexual interactions involving children with peers or younger children is problematic if the relationship is coercive, exploitive, or aggressive or threatens the physical or psychological well being of either participant."[12]

Abuse always affects a person negatively, while flirting is often affirming or flattering to an adolescent. The following chart by Fried and Fried illustrates the dramatic differences between normal sexual behavior between teens and abusive conduct.[13]

Sexual Harassment	Flirting
Makes the receiver feel:	
Bad	Good
Angry	Happy
Sad	Flattered
Ugly	Attractive
Powerless	In control
Results in:	
Negative self-esteem	Positive self-esteem
Is perceived as:	
One-sided	Reciprocal
Demeaning	Flattering
Invasive	Open
Degrading	Complimentary
Is:	
Unwanted	Wanted
Power-motivated	Equality-motivated
Illegal	Legal

In a 1993 study, a stunning 85 percent of girls and 76 percent of boys reported being sexually harassed at school.[14] Eighty-two percent of these incidents were perpetrated by a peer student. Being sexually harassed results in extreme feelings of embarrassment, self-consciousness, loss of confidence, and even skipping school to avoid further harassment.

The South Washington County Schools, a school district in Minnesota, developed a helpful listing of behavioral criteria defining harassment for their schools:

1. Student bra snapping, giving "snuggies," or "pantsing" (pulling down boys' or girls' pants or pulling up girls' skirts).
2. Students "rating" other students [according to physical appearance].
3. Students displaying or circulating centerfolds or sexually explicit materials.
4. Name-calling: "slut," "whore," "fag," "lesbian," "cow," or "dog."
5. Teasing students about their sexual activities or lack of sexual activity.
6. Students wearing sexually offensive T-shirts, hats, or pins.
7. Displays of affection between students (i.e., "making out" in the halls).
8. Suggestive comments about apparel.[15]

Although not included on this list, these could be added: grabbing breasts, buttocks, or genital areas (often in crowded hallways), deliberately bumping into or brushing up against these areas of another student, or setting up sexually humiliating situations. (Chapter 7 and the Appendix will elaborate on a number of interventions and resources for teachers that have reduced the frequency of sexual harassment and abuse in a number of schools around the country.)

WE CAN MAKE A DIFFERENCE

It is clear that bullying is a significant and pervasive problem for our children. But what I would like to make even clearer is that there is reason for hope. By acknowledging and dealing appropriately with these bullying behaviors, we can dramatically decrease their frequency and harm.

In the 1970s, Dan Olweus organized a nationwide campaign in Norway's schools (grades 1–9) to deal with bullying. Two years after the program began, a study of over forty schools revealed a 50 percent decrease in the frequency of bullying. They also saw a decline in theft, vandalism, and truancy during that time. In addition, students reported higher satisfaction with school life.[16]

These types of programs can make all the difference in the world in the lives of our children. Of course, it takes energy and time to get the tools in place, but then again, that's why you're reading this book, isn't it?

Chapter Two
Who Are The Bullies?

A man's reputation is the opinion people have of him;
his character is what he really is.

—Jack Miner

"I guess I was a bully, a young punk," confesses a suburban high school student. "There was this kid that I picked on relentlessly freshman year. He was a nerd. I didn't like him that much. I would get in his head every day and mess with him verbally. My friends dared me to pour honey in his hair, which I did at lunchtime. He pushed me and I pushed back. We got into a fistfight. I got suspended from school for five days. Since his mom was my mom's friend, he came over and asked if I would forgive him even though I was the one who should have asked him for forgiveness. I felt like an idiot. I stopped picking on him after that."

A fourth-grade girl was walking home with her best friend and another quiet girl she knew. The best friends started throwing snowballs at each other and then turned on the quiet girl who cried for them to stop. Next they smothered the girl's face in snow and left her alone, crying. What had come over them?

An athletic upperclassman was walking by a smaller-than-average freshman and suddenly body slammed him into the lockers. Everyone laughed, so he and his friends did it again the next day and threw more taunts at their victim. After months of this treatment, the victim couldn't take it anymore, and in April 1999, he brought a gun to school and killed one classmate and injured another.

CHARACTERISTICS

Where do bullies come from? Are they born or made? Is there a certain type of child who becomes a bully? If you read many stories about bullying, you will find the vast majority of them are about victims. Very few articles and books take us into the heads of the bullies.

Yet the personality characteristics of the bully tend to be more consistent than the traits of either victims or bystanders. Studies reveal that bullies appear to derive satisfaction from inflicting injury and suffering on others and seem to have little empathy for their victims.[1] Typically a bully is physically bigger and stronger than his victims. The bully is a child who perpetually displays bullying behaviors toward others. In addition, the bully is commonly defiant or oppositional toward adults (teachers, parents, anyone in authority), frequently breaks school rules, and is antisocial.[2]

One characteristic of a bully is that he or she displays a powerful inability to recognize his or her impact on others. Attention Deficit Disorder (ADD) and Attention Deficit Hyperactivity Disorder (ADHD) are biochemical disorders of the brain that increase the likelihood that a child will be inattentive, impulsive (not thinking before he or she acts), or hyperactive (constantly moving). Some studies indicate that children with ADHD or other impulsive disorders may be more prone to becoming bullies.[3] The behavioral problems that attend ADHD are often perceived by other kids as attempts to instigate conflicts. Researcher John Lochman, Ph.D., even discovered that most bullies consistently perceive other kids as more aggressive than they are.[4]

Martin, for example, was hyperactive, which irritated everyone around him. He could never sit still, would blurt out things that most kids would never dream of saying, and would lash out at other kids for almost no reason. Martin was both a victim and a bully. His hyperactivity irritated bigger, stronger kids, and they made fun of his "stupidity" and pushed him around. Martin retaliated by turning on someone smaller and quieter, usually one of the learning disabled students in his classes.

Another important characteristic of bullies is their language style. Researcher Robert Selman, Ph.D., found that bullies think and speak in a unilateral manner. Simple one-way commands, demands, and directives make up much of their speech with peers. Normal peer interaction involves a more mature form of communicating that is bi-directional. The mutual exchange of ideas, problem-solving, and generating alternatives typifies this more sophisticated communication and naturally diffuses power struggles through win-win negotiation.[5]

Serious bullies often exhibit antisocial characteristics. *Antisocial* is actually a clinical term in psychology with a specific meaning. Antisocial personality style does not mean, as commonly thought, that the person does not like to be social. Rather, it consists of a cluster of characteristics whose hallmarks are deceit and manipulation.

Additional traits of the antisocial personality style include ignoring the basic rights of others, having a chronic disregard for social norms, being indifferent to the needs of others, blaming victims, and lacking remorse.[6] The modern bully is not typically the lone, overweight, socially awkward boy of our stereotypes, especially those in middle school and high school. Today he is typically the slick power monger, a leader of the pack, looking for targets and gaining popularity points through intimidation. Other kids back off and at times admire the bully's ability to manipulate and control others. "Bullies learn rapidly that aggression works for them" in gaining power and intimidation in the group and, consequently, their behavior becomes self-reinforcing.[7]

Bullies achieve less academically, socially, economically, and occupationally and generally remain bullies throughout their lives.[8] They continue to solve their problems through physical violence toward others whether that person is a peer, spouse, or child of their own. Young bullies carry a one-in-four chance of having a criminal record by age thirty, often for assault or property damage."[9] Even if they do not develop a criminal record, bullies are often "essentially school and job failures due to impulsivity, lack of emotional intelligence, and lack of willingness to conform to the rules and expectations of any given situation.[10]

David is an example of a bully grown up. He was raised by wealthy parents. His father owned a computer chip factory. As a child he almost always got what he wanted, and if he didn't he would try intimidation. With kids at school this often worked. If he got himself into trouble, his parents would get him out of it. No one wanted to stand up to his powerful family.

As an adult, David and his sister inherited their father's business. Gradually, David forced his sister to relinquish control until, by misrepresenting her to the board, he was able to have her removed. He bullied others at work. Any employee who didn't please him was immediately fired. He sexually harassed the women employees, threatened to turn illegal aliens hired as janitors in to the immigration department if they complained about anything, and even got into fist fights with his own managerial staff. His marriage did not last, and he ended up estranged from his children. Although outwardly a financial success, his lifelong pattern of bullying made him a failure in virtually every interpersonal area.

SELF-CONCEPT

The bully's self-esteem has become a controversial topic among researchers. The results of studies are unclear. The prevailing wisdom about self-esteem of bullies is that it is low and distorted, which is often attributed to the poor home environment and their lack of good nurture. In contrast, some studies indicate that "bullies appear to have little anxiety and to possess strong self-esteem. There is little evidence to support the contention that they victimize others because they feel bad about themselves."[11]

The crux of this debate rests on how self-esteem is measured. If it is measured by self-report—that is, the bully's reporting remorse about his bullying behavior toward the victim and reporting feelings of low self-esteem—then the bully is going to appear to have good self-esteem. The bully is often proud of himself for clobbering another kid, because, to the bully, it means that he is better and, therefore, acceptable. If some bullies are truly antisocial or have a deep-seated personality problem, it is only logical and expected that they would not experience remorse.

By nature, though, self-esteem carries with it the ability to show empathy toward others. To truly love oneself, one must also love others. Many psychologists interpret the power-hungry sense of bravado as a façade for a bully's underlying sense of worthlessness that is based on external comparisons and competition.

True self-worth is an internal sense of intrinsic value that is typically learned from parents. According to Christian tradition, being created in the image of God imbues each of us with immeasurable worth to God. This truth is rarely fully grasped in the course of a lifetime. Yet as parents, verbally valuing our children, holding them, and cherishing them as gifts from God, even when they are driving us crazy, can be one of the most empowering gifts we can give our children to face bullies. The internal knowledge that we instill in them contrasts with the hurtful way they are being treated, and they deal with the situation instead of accepting it. (See Appendix E for a checklist on self-esteem.)

Dietzel suggests that our birthright leads us to "become all we can, to be protected from people who do not love themselves, be respected and loved even when we make mistakes, have our strengths emphasized, our weaknesses minimized, and be happy, joyful, and peaceful."[12] While this is idealistic, it speaks to an internalized sense of identity and self-worth versus the superficial definition of self-respect from which some of the researchers were operating.

TYPES OF BULLIES

Dodge & Coie (1987) developed a typology system for bullies.[13] They describe two kinds of bullying: reactive and proactive.

The *reactive* child is constantly on alert, hyper-vigilant to the next perceived wrongdoing that is headed his direction. He is impulsive. Because of a distorted, suspicious perception of the world, he or she retaliates against normal accidents or errors by others as if they were major military assaults. For example, a student who accidentally picks up a reactive bully's folder is likely to get it ripped out of her hands and get pushed to the floor.

The *proactive* bully is the cold, calculating, over-controlled child. This bully is solely focused on power and domination. The bully believes that he is better than others if he has controlled someone weaker. This type of bullying comes out of nowhere for the victim. It is confusing as well as humiliating because the source of the conflict is not interpersonal and is therefore baffling to the victims.

FAMILY ENVIRONMENT

Studies indicate that bullies often come from homes where physical punishment is used, where the children are taught to strike back physically as a way to handle problems, and where parental involvement and warmth are frequently lacking.[14] In fact, most bullies are simply emulating parents who use physical force to get their way.[15] Others are trying to compensate at school for what they suffer at home.

Nick's mom had left when he was little, and his dad was just barely holding things together in their home. His dad yelled at him and sometimes hit him for no apparent reason. Nick could never quite predict how his dad would react to things. He felt powerless. So, at school he created an environment where *he* had the power and control. He had a group of friends around him constantly, and together they picked out victims to torment. Everyone was afraid of them. They got free lunches and free homework assignments by forcing other students to give them up.

Many bullies have been physically abused at home. Psychologist Nathaniel Floyd, Ph.D., discovered that bullies perceive vulnerable children at school as feeling the same way that the bully does at home. Observing vulnerability in another student triggers the bully to feel exposed and threatened and reminds him of the "shame and humiliation of his own victimization."[16] This insight is deep and intuitively precise. It explains the intense and personal drive the bully has to stalk his victim. In the beginning the bullying is personal but only for the bully. It becomes personal for the victim when the shame is transferred to him through the act of bullying.

In addition to abuse, a bully is often neglected emotionally and spends much time unsupervised. A bully frequently observes domestic violence directed at his or her mother from either the father or a boyfriend. Guidelines regarding behavioral expectations are unclear. Discipline is often arbitrary and inconsistent. The same misbehavior can one day yield disproportionate wrath and the next day be completely overlooked. This deadly pattern of punishment creates fear, hopelessness, and depression in children.

A disproportionate number of the kids who were part of the rash of school shootings the last several years were from divorced homes. Trauma at home can easily have direct consequences on behavior at school, even religious schools. (See Appendix C for more characteristics of those who commit school violence.)

Two brothers at a private parochial elementary school started to get into trouble. They had always been well-behaved kids, but now they were habitually bad mouthing, pushing, and hitting other students. When the principal investigated further he discovered that the boys' parents were in the midst of a vicious custody battle in a divorce case.

Dr. Richard Goldbloom explains what the research reveals about the bully's home life:

> Researchers, led by Kris Bosworth of the University of Arizona, collected information from 558 students in grades 6 to 8, then divided the students into three groups: 228 who rarely or never bullied anyone; 243 who reported a moderate level of bullying; and 87 who reported excessive amounts of bullying. Those who reported the most bullying behavior had received more forceful, physical discipline from their parents, had viewed more TV violence and showed more misconduct at home. Thirty-two percent lived with a stepparent, and 36 percent lived in a single-parent household. Bullies generally had fewer adult role models, more exposure to gang activity and easier access to guns. This partly explains why bullies need help as much as victims: Many learn their behavior by example.[17]

Not everyone can be a bully and not every bully will be one all the time. While all children can at times be cruel to one another, bullies make it a habit. But it is a habit that sometimes can be broken. Even more importantly, the scope, impact, and opportunity for bullies can be greatly reduced through strong antibullying policies, as we will see.

Chapter Three
Victims and Bystanders

> In the end we will remember not the words
> of our enemies but the silence of our friends.
>
> —MARTIN LUTHER KING, JR.

Frank Peretti is widely known for his best-selling novels *This Present Darkness* and *Piercing the Darkness*. But now he has written about his own victimization as a child. In *The Wounded Spirit*, Peretti tells a wrenching tale of his school experiences. Because of a birthing defect, Peretti's physical development was delayed, and he had an enlarged tongue that slurred his speech. Basically, he was smaller than other kids and he talked funny. The teasing began in kindergarten, and the torments increased in intensity as he grew up. "I was pushed, shoved, thrown, hit, insulted, badgered, manhandled, teased, and harassed. . . . Increasingly, through the eyes of others, I saw myself as a monster."[1] Peretti explains how he came to think that he deserved the mistreatment and so assumed the school authorities would not do anything about it, which, for the most part, they didn't.

Peretti's narrative helps adults recapture what the world

looks like to a victim of bullying: "As far as I, the timid, obedi-ent, little kid, could see or understand, my parents said I had to be there [at school], the teachers implied through inaction that it was okay for me to be tormented, and the unwritten, anti-snitching law among the kids warned me that I dare not tell anyone. I resigned myself to enduring the abusive behavior of the bullies."[2]

Peretti eventually turned around his school experience through the intervention of some caring staff members at school. That did not happen, however, for Dawn-Marie Wesley of Mission, British Columbia. On November 10, 2000, the fourteen-year-old girl hung herself in her bedroom. In a note to her family, she wrote, "If I try to get help, it will get worse. They are always looking for a new person to beat up, and they are the toughest girls. If I ratted, there would be no stopping them. I love you all so much!" In her case, we see the same "victims' logic" but with a much more tragic result.[3]

Bullying has serious repercussions for its victims. According to a summary of the current research by Ron Banks, "Victims often fear school and consider it to be an unsafe and unhappy place. As many as 7 percent of America's eighth-graders stay home at least once a month because of bullies. The act of being bullied tends to increase some students' isolation because their peers do not want to lose status by associating with them or because they do not want to increase the risks of being bullied themselves. Being bullied leads to depression and low self-esteem, problems that can carry into adulthood."[4] Being victimized can also lead to a deep sense of having done "something wrong to deserve it," or it can cause victims to question life and God, wondering why the bullying is even occurring. Some Christian kids become overwhelmed with doubts about God and why he allows suffering to continue.

Other Christian kids find more and deeper faith through their suffering and discover that God will bring them through it.

At the same time, identifying and working through the social dynamics can greatly lessen the significance and severity of the experience. As Peretti discovered, finding a caring adult who is willing to step into the situation can make all the difference.

This chapter will focus on victims and bystanders, the impact bullying has on each group, and the warning signs that indicate whether your child is a victim of bullying.

VICTIMS

Who are the victims of bullying? Is there a character profile of victims, or is it random, a matter of someone's being in the wrong place at the wrong time? The answer is a little bit of both—which may explain why bullying is so hard to combat.

Is the victim "asking for it"? In a limited number of cases, certain types of victims are instigating conflict unknowingly. When they do so, they perceive themselves as attempting to protect themselves. For the most part, however, bullying is initiated by the bully—and in all cases, the bully is fully and completely responsible for his or her actions.

Talking about traits or characteristics of bullying victims runs the risk of implying that these traits cause or invite the bullying. That is simply not true. Instead, it means that bullies hone in on certain characteristics, because these attributes in the victims increase the likelihood of a bully's success. For instance, victims tend to be physically weaker than bullies. Kids that are anxious, insecure, have poor social skills, or have difficulty making or sustaining friendships are particularly vulnerable to bullying. They tend to be more isolated, are less able to defend themselves, and don't have a support network who will protect them.

Types of Victims

Most researchers have categorized victims into two types: *active* and *passive*. Passive victims, also called "low-aggressive" victims,[5] are described as anxious and insecure. These children consistently do nothing to invite the bully's aggression, nor do they try to defend themselves or confront their attackers. These kids may be physically weaker and emotionally more sensitive. Michelle is such a child. She was born with cerebral palsy and uses a walker at school. She is also from a minority ethnic group and is adopted—two more strikes against her. She is a friendly child who seems to like school and gets along well with adults. But she is often the target of bullies in the hallway. The school has considered giving her a head start each passing period so that she gets to her next class before the hallways get crowded. But this would just further stigmatize her. Instead, some peers are now working on putting together an informal committee of kids who will stand by her if bullies approach to make it clear that she is not alone.

On the other hand, active or "high-aggressive" victims are described as "hot-tempered and restless."[6] Other researchers call these high-aggressive victims *provocative*. They may be diagnosed as learning disabled (LD) or ADHD, and so have poor impulse control. Provocative victims are restless and irritable and often tease or pick on others without realizing the negative impact of their behavior.

Paul, a seventh grader at a suburban middle school, describes a provocative victim, Scott. "Some kids just ask for trouble when they get in a bully situation, like this kid, Scott, in my gym class. He doesn't have any friends even though he's gone to the school for a long time. Scott's a loner. He tries to get attention by getting in trouble and in fights. He gets into fights a lot. Some kids were picking on him in the locker room. The bullies would just come up behind him and try to push him over when he was trying to change his pants. It got so bad that there was a fistfight in the locker room. Now the gym teacher is watching in the boys' locker room so they don't try anything. Some of the kids got detention for picking on him so they stopped. But sometimes he just asks for trouble. Once he was changing clothes in front of my locker and I said, 'Could you move over? I'm trying to get at my gym locker,' and he tried to make a big deal about it and he said, 'You want to fight?' I've never bothered him and yet he was giving me attitude."

Sometimes provocative victims perceive problems when there aren't any. In this situation, it's logical that Scott was tense with Paul because other kids in the locker room were trying to set him up to get mad because they knew they could. However, differentiating bystanders from foes is an important social skill that some kids lack.

Warning Signs

How can parents know if their children are the victims of bullying? Barry McNamara, who teaches in the School of Education at Dowling College, and Francine McNamara, a school social worker, have developed a checklist of warning signs to help parents determine if their child is being bullied.

1. Coming home from school with torn or disordered clothing, or with damaged books.
2. Having bruises, injuries, cuts, and scratches that can't be explained.

3. Not bringing home classmates or other peers after school and seldom spending time on the playground or in the homes of classmates.
4. Not having a single good friend.
5. Seldom or never being invited to parties and not being interested in arranging parties.
6. Appearing afraid or reluctant to go to school in the morning, having a poor appetite, repeated headaches, or stomach pains (particularly in the morning).
7. Choosing an "illogical" route for going to and from school.
8. Having restless sleep with bad dreams or crying in their sleep.
9. Losing interest in schoolwork and getting lower grades.
10. Appearing unhappy, sad, depressed, or showing unexpected mood shifts with irritability and sudden outbursts of temper.
11. Requesting or stealing extra money from family (to give to bullies).[7]

If your child displays some of these signs, avoid direct questions about bullying, since children are often reluctant to talk about it. Inquire instead into how he or she is spending free time at school. Listen to determine whether your child is avoiding peers. Ask who the child might want to invite over after school to build relationships.

Bullying Hot Spots

Almost all bullying occurs at school, and not just anywhere at school—bullying typically occurs where there is no adult supervision. The playground, bathrooms, locker rooms, hallways, parking lots, and buses are all prime locations for bullying.

An effective deterrent to bullying is to minimize its opportunities. One example was the step taken by a suburban Midwestern school, where they put video cameras on all their buses. The cameras record a day's worth of activities. If a student complains of being harassed on the bus, the tape is pulled and viewed. If there are no complaints, the tape records over itself for the next day. Before the video cameras, school administrators claimed that 90 percent of their bullying happened on the bus. Now virtually none occurs on the bus.

Characteristics of Victims

Bullies seem able to select their victims with great precision, focusing on those who are unpopular and vulnerable.[8] Students who are victims of bullying are typically anxious, insecure, and cautious and suffer from low self-esteem, rarely defending themselves or retaliating when confronted by students who bully them. They may lack social skills and friends, be new to the school, and they are often socially isolated.

The major defining physical characteristic of victims is that they tend to be physically weaker than their peers.[9] There is disagreement in the research as to whether other physical characteristics, such as weight, dress, or wearing eyeglasses, correlate with victimization or not.

Still, these characteristics merely increase the likelihood of someone's being bullied. Those who do not share these characteristics are not necessarily free from the potential of being bullied. One example of bullying where the victim was the quarterback of the school football team was featured on a national talk show. He told about how his teammates stripped him of his clothes; taped his hands, feet, and genitals to a pole; and then brought a female student in to have a look.

The parents, outraged, confronted school authorities. The superintendent decided to cancel the school's participation in the regional play-offs to "punish the team"—without first getting input from other school staff. Instead, this secured the quarterback's status as a target. Football parents are often heavily invested in their kids' season, so the result was that the school community ostracized both the boy and his parents, saying it was all just "a locker room prank." When the quarterback refused to apologize to his teammates (for what?), he claims the coach kicked him off the team. While the student obviously suffered from gross abuse, some parents and school officials were completely unable to see it. The quarterback clearly does not fit the portrait of the physically weak, socially insecure, and isolated kid. Anyone can be a victim.

Self-Concept

Victims of bullying demonstrate "fear, anxiety, social isolation, loss of productivity in school, psychological distress, lowered self-esteem, increased school absences, and lower grades."[10] Research indicates that all these problems are compounded when adults do not intervene. The longer the bullying persists, the deeper the wounds and the longer the recovery.

Low self-esteem is almost always evident when kids are in situations of ongoing harassment, such as domestic violence. It creates a cycle of abuse. "The low self-esteem, fear, and anxiety are reinforced so frequently that the pattern is difficult to break. Over time, victims begin to believe that they deserve this mistreatment," write the McNamaras.[11] The self-loathing is communicated from bully to victim, and sometimes the victim becomes a bully to retaliate and seek revenge for what was done to him.

At one school the officials looked out for Julia. From kindergarten to fourth grade she had been one of the bullies' main targets. She would get pushed, her books would get knocked out of her hands, and few kids talked to her at lunch. Then in fifth grade something changed. Julia started hanging out with a large girl in the class who was known as a bully. Soon Julia and her friend were knocking other kids down and throwing their books around. Julia had learned a new coping strategy: She became a bully.

Dr. Tonja R. Nansel reports, "It's likely that kids who are socially isolated and have trouble making friends are more likely to be targets of bullying. In turn, other kids may avoid children who are bullied, for fear of being bullied themselves."[12] Bystanders can be a significant part of the problem and also a significant part of the solution, which will be addressed shortly.

The cycle of abuse was painfully displayed when Charles Andrew Williams showed up at his Santee, California, school with a gun and killed two students and wounded thirteen others. Before the incident, Williams could have been a poster boy for victims of bullying. A transfer from out of state, he was often picked on and punched, and he responded passively to his antagonists. A child of divorce with little adult supervision, he had few outlets for dealing with what was happening to him. That is, until the day in March 2001 when he decided to do some bullying of his own.

Was he a bully or was he a victim?

The National Institute of Health reports that "both bullies and those on the receiving end of bullying were more likely to have difficulty adjusting to their environment both socially and psychologically. Students who were bullied reported having greater difficulty making friends and poorer relationships with their classmates. They were also much more likely than other students to report feelings of loneliness."

The issue of victims-turned-bully is controversial, in that researchers argue that while kids like Williams were once victims, if you look deep enough you will find that many kids like him have indeed engaged in bullying activities with others in lower grade levels. It is often not as simple as saying that bullying someone turns the person into a bully, but it can be a significant cause.

Family Environment

Victims come from all different family environments, running the full spectrum, whereas families of bullies are more uniform and have a more negative family environment.

Some studies indicate that victims of bullies tend to be close to their parents and may have parents who are "overprotective."[13] Some victims' parents rush in to solve their child's problems for them and so inadvertently undermine the child's opportunity to learn the skills needed to resolve conflicts. One parent reports having rushed to her first-grader's side when she saw a larger girl push her daughter into the snow. Towering over the bully, the mother threatened, "If you ever touch my child again, I'll come back and knock your block off!" That little display of temper on the mom's part may have relieved her daughter of one bully, but it taught her nothing in the long run and just confirmed that might makes right.

At the same time, before you resolve to never interfere with your child's life, there is an opposite problem to being overprotective: being underprotective. Some parents of victims remain uninvolved with their kids and do not step in to advocate with the schools when their kids have truly exhausted all their own resources and need adult help. Frank Peretti in *The Wounded Spirit* reports on how often he was told to "just ignore" the bully. That lack of response to his pain convinced him that he would never be able to find relief from the boys that tormented him. That's what can happen when parents are inattentive.

Since we are human, and therefore have both a created and *fallen* nature, it is difficult to figure out this balance. Like many other aspects of parenting, there are times to empower and teach, there are times to let go and let your children fly solo, and there are times where you need to step in and protect them. The trick is figuring out which to do when.

Another factor that influences the effects of bullying is how well the parents model the virtue of showing respect to one another. If a bullying victim is used to disrespect at home, he or she will be more likely to believe the disrespect he or she receives from the bully. As parents, we must guard our tongues, making sure not to perpetuate negative expectations for our children. Common examples of modeling disrespect include the following:

- "Why didn't you do as well on your report card as Billy?" (negative comparison)
- "You never pick up after yourself." (superlative language)
- "You're never going to amount to anything." (negative prediction)
- "You're lazy and a loser." (name calling)
- "Do your chores, now!" (direct orders, versus respectful language)
- "I don't want to hear what you think. Just do what I say." (devaluation of kid's perspective)
- "Stop crying and act like a man." (discrediting emotion, reinforcing emotional shutdown, gender locking)

These are just a few of the many ways we disrespect our children. One check on the language you use with your children is to imagine saying the same phrase with the same tone of voice to an adult. If it seems out of line with an adult, it is likely to be inappropriate with your child as well.

BYSTANDERS

An often overlooked aspect of bullying is the effect it has on bystanders. Most kids in school have been a bystander to a bully event at one time or another. A study conducted by Charach, Pepler, and Ziegler found that 43 percent of students said that they would try to help the victim; 33 percent said that they should help but do not; only 24 percent said that bullying was none of their business.[14] Since the majority (76 percent) of students either do intervene or feel they should in bullying situations, working with the bystanders is a natural way of positively intervening in bullying.

One middle school in the Detroit area realized that the students knew much more than staff about what was happening at the school. They instituted a schoolwide system that let kids know they could report bullying anonymously and confidentially. Soon after, two students let the assistant principal know that there was going to be a fight between two girls after school and that all the students were talking about it. The assistant principal told the principal, but he did not say who had told him. The students' identities were protected. At the same time, staff met with students throughout the afternoon and averted the situation before someone got hurt.

Tapping into the resources and information of the general student population can go a long way in minimizing the harm caused by bullies.

Self-Concept

Dr. Richard Goldbloom writes, "Most bullying takes place in and around school and is often reinforced by an audience. In one study, 120 hours of video surveillance in Toronto schools showed that in over 20 percent of bullying, peers actively reinforced bullying by physically or verbally joining in the aggression. In 54 percent of cases, they reinforced the bully by watching but not joining in. In only 25 percent of cases did peers support the victim."[15] For many kids watching a bullying incident—whether or not they participate—creates an internal moral crisis. Questions arise in the child's conscience, such as, "Am I a bully too?" "Why couldn't I defend that victim in front of others?" "Why did I cheer when I knew it was wrong?" "Am I evil?" These are loaded issues that can have significant implications for future moral development, depending on how they are answered and processed.

Characteristics

Bystanders come in three types: Silent, Instigator, and Challenger.

Silent bystanders will just keep quiet and thereby passively give consent to what they see happening before them. This silence most often stems from fear that the violence will be turned on them if they intervene. Silent bystanders may be seriously traumatized by the bullying but are seldom seen as having anything to do with the incident. While it would be great to enable Silent bystanders to become more active warriors against bullying, the reality is that most will not put themselves at risk. That is why bullying programs must provide risk-free ways for bystanders to report what they know and saw.

This should be coupled with schoolwide seminars that help students understand the difference between "reporting" and "tattling" and provide them with a wide range of easy-to-use strategies for bullying situations. For instance, just getting kids to walk away from a bullying incident versus watching and thereby giving attention, and thus reinforcement, to the bully would be an improvement. As part of the program, role playing and processing situations together with peers will help them think through ahead of time what their response should be. (See chapter 4 for more ideas of what bystanders can do.)

In addition, bystanders can be seemingly identical to the bullies themselves, thus being *Instigators*. These kids activate and escalate bullying. "I dare you to . . ." often leads a kid to go against his own better judgment and do something foolish and even lethal. The nine-year-old boy who was jumping on a frozen lake with his friend when the ice cracked is a horrifying example. The ice held. The boy sighed with relief. The other boy said, "I dare you to jump again," and the boy fell through the ice and died of hypothermia within minutes.

Bullying takes on a mob mentality when the challenge, or dare, is in front of a group of friends. "Grab him, get him, get his pants!" can lead to assault in no time. The risk of losing face in front of friends creates more peer pressure than some kids know how to handle. They cave in to the pressure and make poor and sometimes dangerous decisions. That is how seemingly good kids can end up doing horrible things.

Dan, a sixteen-year-old guy who is over six feet tall, popular, and attractive, attends a suburban high school. He described how his girlfriend became a participant with the bullies. "I was at a party with my new girlfriend, Lindsey. She said Tim, her ex-boyfriend, was outside and that he was looking for me." This comment, or dare, makes her an Instigator, since she knew Tim had a reputation for drunkenness and getting into fights. Dan went outside to "check it out." The next thing he knew he was being grabbed and carried by four of Tim's friends about a quarter mile down the road near a ravine. They threw him on the ground. While his friends egged him on, Tim hit Dan over the head with a rock three times. Car lights stopped the incident as a person headed for the party drove by and stopped. The boys fled. The driver was afraid of retaliation so drove on to the party and called the police anonymously. Dan's sister was at the party, and the driver went up to her and said, "Your brother got beat up pretty bad; you better go see." Tim was charged with assault, the other boys with accessory charges. Dan and his family were astonished that the boys' parents did not make the boys apologize for the hospitalization and the concussion they had caused. Fellow students were unsympathetic to Dan. Even after the incident, it was a long time before Dan could see that his girlfriend had set him up for the beating based on her romanticized idea of the incident as "boys fighting over me."

The final type of bystander is the *Challenger*. This type of bystander has usually been bullied in the past. But they have worked through the intimidation of being bullied and feel confident in their internalized sense of self to be able to deflect and disregard negative comments. Maggie, a high school senior, went through tough times with bullies in sixth grade. Now she says, "When I see kids picking on other kids at school, I just say, 'Knock it off! What's your problem?' They come back with comments, but I don't even hear them. I don't care. It's not right. Usually the kid I help will smile at me or say 'Thanks' under her breath." Maggie explains, "I'm with God now. I know he loves me. I couldn't care less what those bullies think of me. I know who I am." The danger for Challengers is putting themselves too much at risk. Again, a bullying program that helps students prepare strategies ahead of time provides Challengers safe options for intervening.

The James H. Bean Elementary School in Sidney, Maine, has an outstanding bystander training program in place. Each year the guidance counselor teaches a third grade unit based on the 1944 Eleanor Estes book, *The Hundred Dresses*. The book tells the story of a popular, wealthy child named Maddie, who picks on an immigrant girl because of her shabby clothes. Maddie's best friend hates watching this behavior and is in a quandary about what to do. The unit focuses on developing alternative behaviors to the dilemma and role-playing them in class. Bystanders are taught that standing up to injustice is important, and they learn what power they have to combat a bully situation.

Bullying not only causes physical and emotional harm, but it also creates moral dilemmas for victims and bystanders alike. It provokes fundamental questions about the worth of those involved and about the goodness and fairness of life.

Chapter Four
What Kids Can Do

Sticks and stones may break your bones,
but shame can really wound you.

Samantha went to a parochial elementary school, where the uniform policy was designed to make everyone equal—but it didn't. "I was a geek. I had big frizzy hair that I hardly ever combed. I had a space between my teeth that my tongue would fit through. I thought I was cool, but I wasn't. I got teased, especially in the beginning of seventh grade. Thank God my one friend Alice stuck by me. Monica was the head of the popular clique. In the hallways they called me ugly and nasty looking. I'd go to the bathroom and just cry for a while. One time, Monica had a party and invited me. She was really nice for a few days ahead of it so I thought, 'Cool, I'm finally in.' At the party, Monica and her best friend, Sarah, called up a guy named Todd on the phone. They all knew I had a crush on him. I was out of the room when they called, and when I walked back in, Monica said, 'Todd's on the phone and wants to know if you'll go out with him,' and she handed me the phone.

"I said, 'Todd, sure I'll go out with you,' and they all burst out laughing. He just hung up. They set me up. I was so humiliated I went home. I decided to change schools after that. I changed to a public school. My neighbor decorated my locker for my birthday. It was so cool. I had real friends. I was more myself and made a lot of friends. Even now I know I'm not the coolest or prettiest, I'm not popular, but I'm respected, and to me that is more important." This type of emotional bullying is all too familiar to many preteens and teens.

This chapter focuses on developing a Christian response to bullying, the common differences between boy and girl bullying, and some suggestions for how kids can respond to bullying by setting verbal, physical, sexual, and relationship boundaries.

WHAT ABOUT THAT OTHER CHEEK?

As we equip our kids to handle bullying situations, we must first evaluate what messages we are sending them regarding bullying. In Christian homes, kids will likely have to wrestle with Jesus' comments on not resisting evil: "You have heard that it was said, 'An eye for an eye and a tooth for a tooth.' But I say to you, Do not resist an evildoer. But if anyone strikes you on the right cheek, turn the other also" (Matthew 5:38–39, NRSV). What does Jesus mean here when it comes to bullies?

Unfortunately, there is not a clear-cut answer to this question. We do know that when others abused Jesus, he chose *consciously* and *actively* not to retaliate. He did not passively "take it" without thinking. He was strong and confident, valuing himself and his role in God's plan, even when he chose not to strike back. Christ even let us know how active this process of restraint was when he counseled his disciples in Gethsemane, "Do you think that I cannot appeal to my Father, and he will at once send me more than twelve legions of angels?" (Matthew 26:53).

How is Christlike obedience different than caving in to a bully's torment? A few characteristics set it apart. It is *active* and *conscious*. Another way to describe it is to say that the motivating drive for Jesus' behavior comes from *within* him versus a helpless response to *external* forces. Just because Jesus' response is internal, active, and conscious does not mean that he takes on any of the responsibility for the abuse. Bullying behavior is completely the responsibility of the bully.

Kids need to pray, talk to friends, parents, and/or other adults to figure out what God is specifically calling them to do to deal with bullies. However, it is vital that they learn that it is important to care for themselves in the process. They are gifts from God for themselves, their family, their friends, and their community. It is not morally right to let an abusive situation continue because of some mistaken notion of martyrdom.

The wounds from bullying are too deep, and an individual's soul is too precious and too important to God to allow a bullying situation to continue. Yet faith demands that we do what is right and that we not return evil for evil. This means we have to find ways to thwart bullying without having to lower ourselves to the bully's moral level.

I asked some Christian kids how being a Christian makes a difference with bullying. Here's some of what I heard: "As a Christian kid, I try not to start rumors or fights and try to be supportive by hanging around and making sure the situation doesn't get too bad for a person [getting bullied]," said Katie, a ninth grader.

One Christian tenth grader, Brian, said about his experiences in a younger grade, "[Kids] hurt my feelings every time they said something. Now that I'm older, they know not to pick on me because I am just as big and as strong as they are. I've been wrestling for the past two years, and the strength I've gained has also helped. I knew that God forgives everyone, and I figured I should do the same."

It is normal that verbal abuse hurts. What is important is to remind your child that the bully's words are either lies or the distortion of the truth. Kids don't need to believe what the bully says. Ask the child, "Does he know you? Does she care about you at all so that you can trust her opinion of you?" Of course not. It is important to train the child to focus on the moral violation of bullying and not on what is said. It is simply wrong and repugnant to God for someone to treat another cruelly. It is the bully who has the problem.

Explain to your child that usually the bully's words have more to do with him than you. He might look really confident, but it's really just an act of "I want to feel superior to you because that is the only way I can feel good about me." Narcissism and solid self-esteem are two very different dynamics.

Families can remind their kids about all their strengths and talents, especially during a bullying time. Family support can combat the low self-esteem generated by verbal abuse. Since this is a time when what other kids think is vitally important, it is hard to fully discount the inane comments of a bully.

One high school senior offered this advice to middle schoolers: "It's really tough. I wasn't very spiritually mature. It takes a lot of courage to stand up and say, 'No, I'm not going to participate in it.' And it takes a lot of wisdom not to believe what the person is saying about you, to stay rational about it. Your natural instinct is to get really upset about it. You don't think, *Oh that's not really true*, even though it's not."

Another message kids get, mostly from their peers, is that

talking to adults never helps. The statistics show that the opposite is true most of the time. Talking to *some* adults doesn't help and can actually hurt. It increases feelings of hopelessness in a child if she talks to an adult, and he does nothing, or if he does something that makes matters worse. However, 85 percent of the time, some type of adult intervention helps to stop a bullying situation. Schools and parents must create situations where kids can be heard and where their confidentiality is assured. Once these conditions are met, many schools have found that the frequency of reporting bullying increases.

Tony, an eighth-grade boy, said, "Christian kids are more likely to tell someone, to try to get help from an adult. They know about trying to work things out."

BULLYING AMONG GIRLS

"Ignoring the inappropriate behavior of your peers is a very effective technique for many behaviors. However, for bullying it doesn't work."[1] The time period between ages nine and fifteen is often very fragile. The shifts in tribal loyalties and heads of groups are almost constant. Social relationships are highly volatile and unstable. It is the developmental time period when kids learn the rules of inclusion in groups. But the social paradigms are shifting from year to year. While it is often unexpected for parents, it is not unusual for some significant changes in friends and groups to take place through the late elementary, middle, and early high school years.

There are a number of differences between boys and girls at this age, which are relevant to bullying. Boys bully more than girls, and the tormenting is more often physical. Debra J. Pepler of York University has reported that 23 percent of boys surveyed said they had engaged in bullying, compared to only

8 percent of girls.[2] Among victims, however, both genders were equally affected.

In addition, males were more likely to say they had been bullied physically (being hit, slapped, or pushed), while females more frequently said they were bullied verbally and psychologically (through sexual comments or rumors). With girls, bullying often takes more subtle forms, such as whispering campaigns, spreading rumors, and shunning—acts designed to destroy friendships.[3] (See Appendix A for excellent resources on friend issues for girls.)

Sally is a junior in high school now but remembers some dark days of junior high. "I would go home every night and cry because I had no friends. I would hear my name as I passed people in the hall. They were always talking about me. My parents didn't ask."

Both girls and boys do gang up for increased bullying impact. One researcher, Margaret Sagarese, the author of *Cliques*, describes the dynamic: "It is a group behavior. It is a group of girls shunning one girl; it can be a look, a word, a tone of voice. Girls use friendship as the currency of bullying, saying, 'You can sit with us today,' and then when you go and sit down tomorrow, they look at you like eeeew. You wonder is it your hair, your outfit, or did you forget to put deodorant on? With boys, it's rumors that you're gay, always something on the manliness rating."[4]

The major difference most researchers found between the genders is that girls engage more in psychological warfare, whereas boys engage more in physical warfare. Manipulation of friendships, social exclusion, spreading rumors of sexual activity, and smear campaigns can all be a part of the female arsenal.

Stan Davis, a guidance counselor at Bean Elementary school

in central Maine, has launched a revolutionary respect program that has transformed the school. Still, he says, he hasn't "licked the problem of pre-adolescent girls and their particular form of exclusionary bullying. There's name calling, harassment, unfriendly demands . . . in subtle shifting ways that are hard to pin down."[5]

One eighth-grade girl describes it this way: "Girls can be really bad. They will make the rest of your social existence miserable, if they can. They will isolate people, just not talk to you, and have their friends not talk to you."

Another middle-schooler explains the girl dilemma: "Confidence is important, but if people are mean to you, it's intimidating. If you are alone, it's hard to stand up for yourself. If they aren't talking to you, you have to hope that there is someone who doesn't care and will talk to you."

As we saw from the opening story in this chapter, sometimes the female ostracism becomes so entrenched and the anxiety it provokes so intense that the best solution may be changing schools.

But schools are not the only places that this sort of bullying takes place. It can be particularly difficult to deal with in church settings because it is so subtle. One high school girl dropped out of her youth group—and almost gave up her faith—after never feeling that she was accepted. "I moved to this city when I was in middle school, and we started going to the church. At first things seemed okay in the youth group in middle school because there was more parental supervision. But when I switched to the high school group in ninth grade, all the cliques reasserted themselves. I was deliberately left out of everything and shunned. The youth director, a young single guy, did not seem to notice what was happening or didn't know what to do about it. Finally, it was too painful to continue. I started attending another, much larger, youth group at another church. There the size and diversity of the group, and the strong leadership by a married couple, seemed to be an antidote to ostracism of newcomers."

The harassment this girl faced at the church was much more subtle than the boys' who would start fist fights with each other and yell insults. As a result, the girls' behaviors were never confronted, and the leadership of the group even blamed this girl for "not trying harder to fit in." In church settings, where people are expected to conform to certain "Christian" behaviors, subtle bullying can be particularly insidious. Leaders must confront this for what it is—unchristian behavior, envy, hatefulness, backbiting, gossip, false witness, and so on.

DEALING WITH SEXUAL HARASSMENT

Girls are more often the target of sexual harassment than boys. A 1993 study by the American Association of University Women found that 76 percent of boys and 85 percent of girls reported being sexually harassed at school. Of those students, 80 percent said the harassment was from a peer.[6]

"Typical" sexual activity among teens can take on bullying aspects. In one large study, 70 percent of high school boys said, "It is okay to lie to a girl about being in love with her in order to get her to have sex."[7] Having explicit conversations with preteens and teen girls to develop a clear set of sexual guidelines and boundaries is a vital part of empowering young girls.

Stanton and Brenna Jones, the authors of *How and When to Tell Your Kids About Sex*, report that Christian girls may feel a stronger sense of social deference to boys if their church background is extremely conservative and patriarchal. An overdeveloped sense of "obligation" that the girl "owes the boy something for having gone on a date with him," can push girls to go against their true wishes with sexual behavior.[8]

Only 10 percent of high school boys believed they would marry the first woman they had sexual intercourse with, whereas over half of the nonvirgin girls surveyed believed they would marry the boy they first had sexual intercourse with. Only 3 percent actually did. With such huge differences in perspectives on sexuality during the middle and high school years, the potential for sexual bullying becomes great. Girls need to be equipped for the task. We will go into more detail later on what boundaries can be established to protect girls.

BULLYING AMONG BOYS

Bullying with boys generally does not involve even a hint of friendship or the lure of it. The bully can be completely unknown to the victim or someone he knows in a minimal way. The enemy status of the relationship becomes outright and obvious early on. It is often the basic physical challenge—who is stronger—and the mental challenge of who is more cunning and callous.

While most books say for kids "not to fight back," the research about early elementary school is mixed on physically taking a stand in self-defense. Since the social scene of early elementary school is often more fluid, flexible, and transient, taking a stand physically does work on occasion.

Tim, a high school senior, reported, "I know you're not supposed to fight back, but when I was in third grade this kid came up and pushed me down three days in a row. I finally got sick of it and pushed back. He fell down but wasn't hurt, but he never messed with me again." Making a physical response, in a self-defensive and not overbearing manner, seemed to stop the bullying in this case. Tim went on to say, "I think that is atypical. In junior high and high school people are more persistent and are more likely to come back at you. They won't let it go." The research seems to agree that physical retaliation tends to escalate conflict.

I came across several accounts, though, of elementary students who physically defended themselves successfully against bullies, but none for older students. Chad, a junior, said, "Do fights stop fights? Not usually. It just makes it worse. Guys like to try to win the fights, and if you come back at them, it's a challenge, and they have to come back at you to stop it."

Some experts claim that the male propensity for trouble is exacerbated by a lack of life training provided by dads and the community. A wonderful resource for providing just that type of training is Robert Lewis's *Raising a Modern-Day Knight: A Father's Role in Guiding His Son to Authentic Manhood* (see Appendix A).

WHAT VICTIMS AND BYSTANDERS CAN DO

Here are some suggestions for how we can equip students to respond to bullying. Which strategy they use will depend on the context of the abuse, but many are good "rules of thumb" for any situation. The first set is what students need to believe in order to respond actively and assertively. Then we will cover skills and strategies that help students establish healthy verbal, physical, relational, and sexual boundaries.

- *Realize that you are not alone.* Bullying can be an isolating experience where the child feels there is no outlet for help. But bullying is a common phenomenon. In his book *The Wounded Spirit,* Frank Peretti explains to bullying victims, "Everybody has something they wish they could change about themselves. If you have discovered some 'defect' in yourself, welcome to the human race. . . . All of us, with all our wrinkles, shortcomings, bumblings, and imperfections, are God's creation. We're all precious in His sight and should be precious to one another—and don't let anyone tell you otherwise, not even you."[9]

- *Realize it is not your fault.* Victims often believe that they deserve the bullying, that it is their punishment for whatever shortcoming they think they have. Again, Frank Peretti describes how he changed his thinking after first believing that he deserved the bullying he received: "It wasn't my fault. What those kids did to me had nothing to do with me. There was never anything so terribly wrong with me that other people had no choice but to be irresistibly, uncontrollably compelled to abuse me. Yes, I was a sinner who needed to be saved by God's grace, but I was not some freak of nature who merited the disdain with which I was treated. It wasn't my problem; it was theirs!"[10]

Active victims, who sometimes have poor impulse control and can play a role in provoking bullying behavior, still should not be held responsible for the bullying itself. The bullying itself is not their fault. Just because a person is irritating to be around does not justify abuse. It is fully the bully's fault and responsibility when he or she engages in abuse.

- *You do not have to believe what people say about you.* Believing those who show malice toward you versus those who care for and support you is simply not rational. Yet that is what many of us do. We need to focus on the positives that we get from friends and family, not on the criticism we receive.

- *Remember, God has a plan for you.* And it is not to be the punching bag of bullies.[11] God loves you, just as you are. Incorporating that perfect love into your life will help you to be strong when others are trying to weaken you.

Setting Verbal Limits and Boundaries

1. Talk about it.

Schools and parents must listen, respect, and respond to what kids tell them. Cindi Seddon, a school principal and cofounder of Bully B'ware Productions, explains that "first and foremost, teachers must make it safe for students to report bullying. It is crucial that teachers, administrators and other school personnel respect the anonymity of the victim and/or reporting students. Until students trust this will happen, bullying will go unreported, and bullies will continue to thrive."[12] Creating an environment for students to report bullying is so important because the most effective intervention against bullying is adult involvement.

2. Identify and use adult allies.

Students need to seek out and initiate contact with those adults they already know and trust or those at school who have a good reputation for listening and responding to students.

3. Develop a sense of humor.

Practice and role play using humor to defuse bullying situations. One ninth grader, who was small for his age and was involved with theater, was often the victim of bullying. He was called "gay," "queen," and "homo" and was often body-slammed into lockers. The school was unresponsive in providing help. So, the boy decided to use his theater experience by using an "improv" acting style and turning slights into jokes. When he was called "queen," he responded by playing the part to an exaggerated degree, drawing applause from the audience of bystanders (who welcomed having a tense situation diffused by humor). He has significantly improved his life at school, though he has not totally eliminated bullying.

4. Call 911 if the situation is really dangerous.

Any child who is seriously threatened should feel free to call 911 and ask for help, even if he or she is inside the school. If school authorities are not responding to stop the abuse, then someone from outside must do so.

5. Be polite but firm.

Tell the bully, "Stop it. I don't like it. Leave me alone."[13] This may sound too easy, but often an assertive verbal reply is all it takes to communicate that, if the problems continue, you will react strongly.

6. Be assertive.

Without responding in kind, there are many ways for students to stand up to the bully, from stating clearly that what the bully is doing is wrong to even more aggressive responses. In sixth grade, Greg was assigned the task of helping another student, Mike, known as a bully, with his math. Mike asked Greg for the answers. Greg explained that he would not give answers because Mike was supposed to learn the math, not just get the answers. Mike told Greg that unless he gave him the answers, now, that he would beat him up. Greg gulped and then assertively told Mike that if he hit Greg then Greg would never again help him with math. Mike said fine and got back to work.

7. Threaten a bully who might back off from a show of strength.[14]

We are not talking about giving the bully a dose of his own medicine. But a child can threaten to turn the bully in or to pursue some other action that would be unpleasant for the bully. Obviously a lot of discernment is needed for when this is appropriate.

8. Use "I" messages.[15]

Limiting your statements to "I think . . ." and "I feel . . ." keeps the focus on the behaviors and the specific situation. Otherwise, conversations can degenerate into name-calling and defensive posturing. "You . . ." messages put people on the defensive and are normally perceived as critical. As a result, the message is lost.

9. Involve a peer mediator.[16]

Many schools have trained older, mature students who can intercede in smaller-scale problems that come up. Often this is a less threatening solution to all involved.

Setting Physical Limits and Boundaries

1. Read and avoid dangerous situations.

Students must learn to trust their instincts for perceiving danger and threat. If they are feeling scared, there is probably a reason for it. They must learn to trust their own instincts, which is often the opposite message from what we teach them. Gavin de

Becker, a security specialist, describes intuition as follows: "Nature's greatest accomplishment, the human brain, is never more efficient or invested than when its host is at risk." As parents we often train our kids not to listen to their instincts, when what they need is the exact opposite.[17] (See Appendix D for a list of things kids should know to protect themselves.)

2. Travel with a group or peer.

Bullies tend to look for "easy" victims who lack someone to support them or back them up.

3. Run away.

If a student is in a threatening situation, there is no shame in acting on self-preservation or self-defense. If a child has strong legs, he or she should use them!

4. Do an appearance check-up.[18]

Make sure the reason for the bullying is not poor hygiene. A parent or friend should help the child assess his or her hair, body odor, clothing status, and posture. The idea is to find a balance between being obsessed by appearance and completely ignoring it. Smelly is "uncool" by any standard. Make sure the outside of the child is conveying the goodness of the whole person as much as possible.[19] In late elementary school and middle school, both boys and girls begin undergoing physical changes. One of these is that the body chemistry changes and perspiration that used to lack an odor now is pungent. This change often takes kids by surprise. They are not prepared for the additional time they need to take at home and after gym to avoid body odor. Parents and teachers can gently remind them about this if they notice that it is a problem. Bad breath, especially when a child has a cold, can be another real "turn off" that will label a child as uncouth.

5. Look the bully in the eye.
Stand straight and tall if faced with a bully.[20] The goal is to show that you are not there to be his punching bag. If at all possible, don't cry or otherwise show you are upset. Walk away if you can't hide your feelings.[21] There's nothing a bully likes better than getting an emotional response from a victim, so stay cool.

6. Fight back as a last resort.[22]
Many children benefit from classes in self-defense or the martial arts.[23] These classes focus on helping children stay calm and focused. They teach skills to use when confronted by a larger attacker. They also develop strength and agility. Lifting weights and getting in shape boost confidence and improve the ability—mentally and physically—to handle threatening situations.

7. Get involved with activities that make you feel good.[24]
Success and mastery in one field often creates self-confidence that carries over into other areas of one's life. If a student excels in something—even a rather unusual hobby—he or she may win respect from peers that will help in social situations.

8. Switch schools.
Although this is a last resort, it should not be completely ruled out. If a child is not fitting in, has been repeatedly humiliated, and has begun to fear school, a switch may be necessary.

Sometimes moving from a private to public school, or vice versa, will help. Just a change of scenery can have an important impact. The child can make a fresh start, perhaps with some new social skills. Although public schools do not like to see students moving from one district school to another, this can be done if the circumstances warrant it.

Setting Relational Limits and Boundaries

1. Have more than one social context.
If things are going poorly at school, a student can look for a church youth group or a special-interest club that will allow him or her to build a fresh network of relationships in a different setting. Once you have a friend in one place in your life, it is often easier to build them elsewhere.

2. Learn new social skills.
Sometimes a student feels friendless and worthless when the problem may be a simple lack of a particular social skill, such as conversing with new acquaintances. Seminars, informal role-plays with family members, or help from the school social worker may be options to remedy this.

Setting Sexual Limits and Boundaries

1. Develop a personal code of sexual behavior.
Students should know their personal limits for physical expression—such as levels of holding hands, hugging, kissing—before they are in potentially compromising situations. They should

also be clear with their dates about the status of the current relationship.

2. Develop guidelines for creating a healthy dating relationship.

Stanton and Brenna Jones suggest the following blueprint for a dating plan for teens:[25]

- "Teens should be accountable to definite plans and guidelines." Specific locations and activities are required while others should be prohibited. Until a child can be comfortable with responsible dating, he or she should not be allowed to date.
- "Couples should avoid sexually explicit media as part of their activities." Parents have to monitor where the teens are and what they are doing.
- "Teens, especially young women, should dress modestly rather than provocatively." This has become increasingly difficult in an era of spaghetti straps and body-fitting material, but perhaps this is an area where we should put a priority on being countercultural.
- "Teens should choose all their companions, especially those they date, very carefully. Our companions will shape who we are (see Proverbs 13:20)."
- "Teens should be prepared to talk openly about sex and their moral standards with the people they are dating."
- "Christian teens can include prayer in dating, both before and during a date."
- "Teens should avoid high-risk situations." These include, but are not limited to, unchaperoned parties, events where drugs and alcohol are consumed, or settings where sexual activity is the norm.

Sexual activity is a particularly problematic area for teens, since they are all still struggling to figure out how relationships and sex "work." These insecurities, combined with the different expectations between boys and girls, can lead to some genuinely confusing scenarios, such as this story from Kevin, a high school junior. He had a friend, Todd, charged with sexual harassment. Todd was with his girlfriend, and they were messing around, and he asked in a vulgar fashion, "Wanna [have sex]?" She said she had to go, and the next day he was arrested for sexual harassment and rape. All the charges were later dropped because Kevin had been there and made it clear that Todd had not forced the girl to have sex. But Todd got a bad reputation for it, and the girl did not seem to understand the critical nature of her accusation.

It is obvious the girl felt threatened and, perhaps, even violated, but Kevin sees his friend as the one violated. Instead of trying to be as wise as Solomon in such situations, it is a better policy to choose your friends carefully and only date those who can sign on to the dating code you want to follow.

What Bystanders Can Do

Even if students are not bullied, there is still plenty they can do in the fight against bullying. By being a friend and showing respect, they can change the environment they live in.

1. Befriend the friendless.

A student does not have to become best friends with social outcasts to improve their lives. A casual greeting and an occasional conversation can communicate to the whole school that this person is more than a target for bullies.

One seventh-grade girl explains her experience and how

she made friends with an unlikely student: "This girl always sat at our table, and no one talked to her. I got sick of it and just started talking to her. She's a little crazy but she's nice. I don't care. The other girls asked me why I talked to her. I told them, 'She is far more interesting than you.'"

2. Don't gossip.
Besides being wrong and prohibited by Scripture (see for example, Proverbs 16:28; 2 Corinthians 12:20), gossip can further relational bullying when gossip is used to keep someone on the "outside." Here is the advice from one veteran of middle school: "Rumors are basically not true. My general expectation is that it's not true. I'd either say nothing back to the person, or if it was a close friend, I might say something back about how the information was probably wrong."

3. Tell someone if you see bullying.
In their book *Cliques: 8 Steps to Help Your Child Survive the Social Jungle*, Charlene Giannetti and Margaret Sagarese offer many helpful suggestions for what bystanders can do to thwart bullies: Don't watch (Bullies love an audience.); don't react (Bullies are looking for support.); offer verbal support in private; offer support to the victim in front of the clique leader; get a teacher or parent involved.[26]

WHAT BULLIES CAN DO TO CHANGE

If you are working with a child who is bullying, the best first step is to apply strong consequences to the behavior and to enforce them consistently. Many schools have a zero-tolerance policy where bullying entails automatic suspension.

If the bully is young or seems open to improving his social skills, a peer support group is often a helpful means to learn the consequences of their behaviors and so develop empathy. It is also an excellent forum for learning new problem-solving skills that can act as an alternative to bullying behaviors.

In their comprehensive work *Bullies and Victims*, experts Suellen and Paula Fried list many of the issues that bullies can work on in groups or on their own:

- Learn how to handle your anger.
- Ask yourself, "Why am I doing this?"
- Get help to feel better about yourself.
- Try to stop picking on someone for just one day.
- Listen to a friend.
- Talk to another bully and discuss your behavior.
- Work really hard to control your behavior.
- Think about how you would feel if you were the victim.
- Try to get attention by doing something good.[27]

In the video *The Wounded Spirit,* Frank Peretti offers a simple three-point plan for bullies: Cut it out, confess your wrongs, and make it right.[28]

Chapter Five
What Parents Can Do

It is easy to be brave from a safe distance.

—AESOP

"**M**y parents didn't push me to talk. They knew that I needed to come to them when I was ready. They listened and reminded me that I was a good person. Then they helped me try to find something to get into that wasn't connected to school or that group, where I could meet new people," explained Katie, a high school student, when asked what her parents did right regarding bullying.

"Sometimes parents try to go in, thinking, *I don't like it when my kid is hurting so I'm going to solve the problem*. But kids will tell you some of what's wrong; they may not tell you everything. The parents should listen to what you say and what you have already tried to do to solve the problem. They shouldn't go in thinking they'll solve everything for you. I wouldn't have gotten where I am if they had done that. I would have been totally screwed up," explained Carol, another high school student, when asked about common problems parents make.

WARNING SIGNS

Parents have to perform a balancing act when dealing with bullying. They cannot be too protective or they risk not teaching their children the necessary coping skills they need to lead independent lives. Some studies seem to indicate that there is a correlation between being a bullying victim and having overprotective parents.[1]

At the same time, parents are responsible for the safety and protection of their children. If their children are being harmed or traumatized, the parents are the number one safety net for their children. It is often up to the parents to become their child's advocate in the educational system to ensure his or her protection.

Complicating matters still further is the fact that teens are highly ambivalent about whether or how much they want to tell their parents. Explains one teen, "I never tell my mom anything. I don't trust her." Another shares, "It's a lot more difficult for guys to talk to their parents about problems. I just suck it up and talk to my friends about them. Guys aren't supposed to cry. I don't talk to my parents. I don't tell my mom anything because I don't want her to come in and fix my problem. I want to fix my problem." Erin offers a female perspective: "When I come home from school, my mom says, 'What's wrong? Tell me.' When I say, 'I don't want to talk about it,' she won't let me be. I wish she'd just listen and wait till I'm ready to talk."

So what is a parent to do? How are we to navigate these issues, keep communication lines open, and deal with a bullying problem?

First things first. The initial task is to discern whether or not your child is a victim of bullying. Kids often will not tell you they are being bullied. Parents need to be proactive. In a *Readers Digest-Canada* article, Dr. Sarah Shea, director of the Child Development Clinic at the IWK Health Centre in Halifax, explained what to look for: "unexplained reluctance to go to school; fearfulness or unusual anxiety; sleep disturbances and nightmares; vague physical complaints (headaches, stomachaches), especially on school days; or belongings that come home ripped or are missing altogether."

Dr. Shea goes on to recommend that you not ask your child outright about bullying. "Ask your child indirectly how he or she is spending the lunch hour; or what it's like walking to school, walking home, or taking the school bus. Ask if there are any children at school who are bullies, without personalizing it. And when you meet with teachers, ask how they deal with conflict when it occurs. If you are certain your child is being bullied, let the school know that you take it seriously, and ask what can be done to help."[2]

Once you know that your child is a victim of bullying, there are several tasks you must do for your child and several common mistakes that you should avoid.

WHAT PARENTS SHOULD DO

1. Wait for the child's timing.

You may figure out something is wrong before your child is ready to tell you. Accept it at face value if the child doesn't want to talk right then. I find that my kids don't say much right after school or during dinner about upsetting events at school. But when the lights are going off, then the hard questions and deep sharing come out. Many families use daily, open-ended investigative questions with their children, such as, "What was the high point and the low point of your day today?" This provides a ritualistic way of talking about negative experiences.

I know one mother who communicates both care and "space" by actively praying for her children and letting them know. According to her daughter, it seems to work: "My mom was in a group of moms that prayed for kids in our high school. She wouldn't pry into my life, but every Tuesday she would say, 'I prayed for you today.' That was very cool."

2. Listen carefully.

So now that you have them talking, make sure you listen. That may sound obvious, but it is easy to jump directly from acknowledgment of the problem to becoming Superparent and immediately proceeding to problem solving. But it is critical that you truly listen to your children. What do they think triggered the bullying? What have they done to try to solve it? What worked and what did not work? What do they think should be done? Asking them questions teaches them that they are full participants in figuring out what to do.

Kelsey, a seventeen-year-old, describes what it is like to have a mom who has learned the art of being a good listener, whether in times of crisis or in everyday life. "I've been blessed by the coolest mom in the world. Everyone calls her Momma Sue. Every night I'll go into her room, sit at the foot of her bed, and I'll just tell her everything, anything that's bothering me. She'll be there for support and advice if I ask for it. She tells me, 'You're almost an adult; so I'm going to let you make your decision, but here are some ideas if you want them.'"

3. Assure your child that it is not his or her fault.

Part of growing up is figuring out how to fit in and get along, and children naturally feel a lot of anxiety about their status.

So if a bully is picking on them, it is easy for them to think that they deserve the harassment. *I must have done something wrong,* they think. You are their reality check. No child deserves to be on the receiving end of malicious acts, and it is the bully who has crossed the line of what is inappropriate behavior.[3]

4. Offer advice only when it is requested.
It is tempting to tell your child what to do and solve the problem for him or her. Don't. Become a partner and wait for your invitation to help solve the problem. You are teaching them a life skill, and you don't want them to miss the lesson on how to deal with bad things in their lives.

Ask your child how you can help at any given point and listen to the answer.

5. Empathize.
Picture yourself in your child's situation and identify the feelings. Try to remember the days when "fitting in" seemed the ultimate purpose in life or when you first had to face an evil force that was focused on you.

6. Validate their experiences.
Many bullying victims tell of times they tried to tell their parents, but their parents refused to take it seriously.[4] Kids need to know that you hear them and believe them—that you, the parent, are the safety net they can go to in times of trouble. Even if the events turn out to be routine peer conflicts, the children will have learned that you take them seriously and are prepared to act to protect them.

7. Help them make friends.
Sometimes a bully can be made into a friend. Jan's daughter,

Lori, was a very small first grader when two older and bigger boys, who lived on the street, started picking on her, both on the playground at school and in the neighborhood. Because she was so young and small, there was little she could do for herself. At first, her dad got involved. He and another dad from the neighborhood, whose kids were also being picked on, visited the boys' home. They found the boys' parents at home, drunk, at 5:00 P.M. on a Friday afternoon. Clearly, the parents weren't going to positively intervene.

Then Jan had an idea. The weather was getting cold, and she often saw the boys walking to school. Many times they were obviously going to be late. One day she decided to offer them a ride when she was driving Lori to school. On the first day, only the younger boy accepted the ride, but she welcomed him into the car. She asked him to stop picking on her daughter and said that she'd be happy to drive him whenever she saw him walking in cold weather. Two days later, his brother joined the ride. She told him the same thing. She became friends with the boys, trying to be a positive influence and role model for them, and they stopped picking on Lori. In fact, in one case they defended Lori when someone else was threatening her on the playground.

If you can't make friends with the bully, then try working through mutual friends. In *The Wounded Spirit*, author Frank Peretti tells a story about his friend Paul. He and Paul both knew another guy who had been tormenting Peretti. To Paul, that other guy was a decent friend. To Peretti, he was a bully. When Peretti mentioned this to Paul, Paul was astounded. He could not imagine his friend being a tormentor. But he must have followed up on it. After that conversation, Peretti was never picked on again by that particular boy. His friend Paul must have interceded for him. The more allies a victimized child has, the easier it is to work around the bullies.

8. Admire and affirm.

Tell your child what you like about the way she is handling the bullying situation. Affirmation is the best reinforcement and encouragement tool you have at your disposal, and victims are often thirsty for it.

9. Empower.

Start with the strategies your child comes up with and think through together how to implement the plan. Help your child avoid the situations that expose him or her to bullying. If it occurs on the way to or from school, find a safe route and arrange for an older companion. Also, point out places the child can go for help. Develop a list of friendly kids and specific strategies for each target time when bullying occurs.

10. Protect and advocate.

In selected situations, especially those circumstances with younger, elementary aged children, it is important for parents to talk with other parents, teachers, and school administrators to improve the situation. Do this in coordination with your child and his or her input. Review the results together.

Part of being your child's advocate may mean contacting your child's teacher, principal, or even the police. As one principal explained, "We can't do anything until we know about it. Please tell the school if your child is having a conflict. We are here to help." (We will get into how to deal with schools more fully in the next chapter.) Keep a written record for yourself of what happened, the times and dates, who was involved, and who was notified.

11. Be open to seeing the whole story.

Because we are so eager to protect our children, parents tend to jump to our children's defense when they are threatened. At the same time, our son or daughter may not have provided the full story on the first telling. One mother went to the school demanding that the boy who hit her son be kicked out of school and arrested. Upon investigation, the school discovered that for years a group of boys, including her son, would provoke a larger and slower schoolmate until he would lose his temper. The thrill was staying just out of his reach when he struck out. Her son was simply too slow that day, but it certainly was not a clear case of a bully and his victim.

WHAT PARENTS SHOULD NOT DO

Many don'ts are obvious. Reread the list above and consider the opposite of each point. For instance, you should not simply take over and solve the problem for your child. The following are some other warnings that parents need to know when their child is in a bullying situation.

1. Don't break confidentiality unless absolutely necessary.

It is vital for you to have an open and trusting relationship with your child. If he or she does not want you to contact others, then respect and follow those wishes if it is at all possible to do so and it is in the child's best interests. Sometimes bullying situations can become dangerous and even life threatening, and you will feel compelled to contact the proper authorities for the sake of your child's safety. Make sure you first explain to your child why it is necessary to break his or her confidentiality. You will have hurt your cause if the consequence of your communication is that your child no longer confides in you about what is going on.

2. Don't tell your child to "hit them back."

Barry and Francine McNamara, authors of *Keys to Dealing with Bullies*, say, "'Hit them back' may be the worst advice of all that parents can give their kids. . . . If these smaller and weaker children try to fight back physically, they will probably lose and encourage the bully to pick on them more frequently. Bullies are very good at picking their victims. If they are able to inflict physical harm and they continue to 'beat up' the victims, the behavior will be reinforced and continue."[5] In younger kids (third grade and below), physically taking a stand without striking back may sometimes serve to thwart more bullying attempts with bullies of the same age. At the junior high level, however, the social pecking order is more established and tenacious. Physical resistance can breed revenge and more attacks. As a rule, physical coercion is not a good problem-solving technique.

3. Don't emotionally crowd out your child's feelings with your own anxiety.

Parents can become very upset and very emotional when they learn that there are people in the world who want to harm their son or daughter. Before they know it, they are speaking and acting based on their anxiety and not on what is best for their son or daughter. They must model the emotional maturity they want their child to emulate. They also must provide a safe, nurturing context for their child to share his or her thoughts and feelings.

PARENTS AS MODELS

The two biggest factors that interfere with most parents' ability to listen and respond well to their kids about bullying situations are anxiety and busyness. When we hear about our kids being picked on, our natural visceral response is to want to pound the bully and talk later. If we're more mature, we might be restrained enough to take a deep breath and just want to lecture the bully about what a loser he or she is! But in reality, as in so much of parenting, we are called to forego our emotional fantasy responses, slow our bodies down, and get in a place where we can be available to listen, help, and believe in our children.

As parents we need to model positive and respectful behavior to our kids. Just as bullies often learn their techniques of verbal and physical abuse from watching their parents, so, too, children of victims look to their parents for how to solve problems, how to respond to threatening situations, how to deal with negative feelings, and how to talk about their enemies. Avoid sarcasm and blaming language with your kids.

In fact, modeling and teaching compassion for others is the best way for making sure our own children don't become bullies. Be aware of how you describe others and what language you use when describing people you are having trouble with. Your kids' eyes are taking in more than you realize.

In an article in *The San Diego Union Tribune*, journalist Jane Clifford talked to Margaret Sagarese, a bullying expert who "urges, begs parents to sit down and talk things over with their kids . . . But she cautions that parents can only teach what they are willing to learn themselves."[6]

As parents we must deal with things we would rather not have to face. Many of the "don'ts" listed above are due to anxiety that has not been modulated by its owner and is simply dumped out to the child or situation. Another complicating factor is the pace and stress of life in the twenty-first century. While we want to hear from our kids about their lives, it can seem like one more problem to deal with after a very long and tiring day. So slow down and listen carefully.

Being open and available and modeling how to treat others and solve problems are all good goals, but by themselves even they will fail if there is not good communication with your child. Margaret Sagarese encourages parents by telling them this story about herself: "We all say, 'Not my child.' I hear it when I do the bully talk with parents. And then I tell them that when my daughter was in fifth grade, she was participating in bullying, not even understanding what she was doing."[7] Sagarese learned that she had not talked enough with her own child.

WHEN TO SEEK CLINICAL INTERVENTION

Often having a close relationship with your child and developing together an action plan will help him or her overcome the bullying problem. Sometimes it is necessary to involve school authorities in order to tackle the problem (which will be discussed more in the next chapter). For some cases, additional outside help is needed for the child to overcome the debilitating effects of bullying.

If your child is withdrawn, seems depressed, makes suicidal comments, and loses interest in his normal activities, call a professional psychologist for an assessment. Do not let pass comments, like, "Why bother with all this anyway? Life stinks. It's just not worth it." Follow up and ask your daughter if she has had suicidal thoughts. Teen suicide went up 300 percent between the 1970s and the 1990s. Many parents are afraid that asking about suicidal thoughts will put the thought into his or her head. That is simply not true. In fact, the opposite is true. Kids who do not feel suicidal will say so quickly; those who do feel suicidal are given permission to unload or reluctantly confess. Then you can get them the help they need from a professional therapist.

If some additional life stress that the family is dealing with is compounding a bullying problem—such as a death, divorce, or major illness in your family in recent months—your child needs your help. Seek an adolescent or family therapist to process through and unpack those compounding issues.

For adolescents who were adopted at birth, identity issues may become more complicated in adolescence. The rejection that comes from bullying can take on an additional sting when unconscious feelings of abandonment are triggered as adult identity formation begins. These are the multilayered issues that a trained therapist can help sort out.

Help is available. As parents, we do not have to do everything on our own. Don't let your own shame or embarrassment prevent you from getting the help you need for your son or daughter.

Chapter Six
What Schools Can Do

Education is simply the soul of a society as it passes from one
generation to another. Whatever the soul is like, it will have
to be passed on somehow, consciously or unconsciously;
and that transition may be called education.

—G. K. CHESTERTON

It was Wear Your Pajamas to School Day at Emerson Middle
School in Minnesota. Zack was the PTA president's kid, and
he was psyched. Zack wore the same cool PJs every boy did, the
flannel baggie bottoms with the band at the waist. But what
Zack didn't foresee was that he should not have brought his
slippers to school.

Zack was a sensitive boy. Other kids had picked up on that.
And Zack's mother, Sally, was protective of her son. She often
micromanaged Zack's problems, but at the same time she was
emotionally present for him.

That day the bullies cornered him in the bathroom and
swiped his slippers. They then stuffed one down the toilet
while calling him a "fag." Zack later showed up in the school
office with a wet slipper in a bag. It now had a bad odor. The
office secretary asked him to fill out a form for the assistant
principal, recording everything that had happened. Given his

current emotional state, the task proved difficult. Zack emotionally fell apart, crying loudly, which made matters worse. None of the adults sat down and talked the incident through with Zack. He asked to go home early, which was approved, but he had to go back to three of his classes to collect his homework.

The next day the school had scheduled a drama company, Bridgework, to come and do a play about bullying. Good timing.

WHY KIDS WON'T TELL

Surveys reveal that students don't believe that telling adults about bullying situations will do any good. Students believe that "adult intervention is infrequent and ineffective, and that telling adults will only bring more harassment from bullies." They add that teachers "seldom or never talk to their classes about bullying" and that the schools treat bullying as "a harmless rite of passage that is best ignored unless verbal and psychological intimidation crosses the line into physical assault or theft."[1]

These attitudes reflect a sense of helplessness, which is often shared by the adults involved. Most educators and parents pull back from involvement with kids as they enter the junior high years.

Parents often emotionally withdraw from their children in the confusing preteen and early teen years. Staying involved becomes logistically much more difficult, and the developmental issues become much more intimidating. Even simple communication can become labored. Parents are rarely welcomed in the middle school classroom. Big events for the kids, such as dances and trips, are the only way to connect.

At the same time, school officials can become overwhelmed by the range of issues they have to contend with, from sharing on the playground to drug addiction and teen pregnancy. The temptation is to focus on the educational issues and take a minimalist approach to the social dynamics among students.

While staying connected with kids is more difficult during this time, for both parents and educators, it is nevertheless still vital for the well-being of the children. Kids need the modeling and the reinforcement for how to treat others with respect. If this ideal is not lifted up at home and at school, then the law of the jungle can take over where the strongest prey on the weakest. But when respect is lifted up as the standard for the school and home, and enforced, great things can be unleashed.

New York City, under the leadership of Mayor Rudolf Guiliani, enjoyed a positive transformation when they instituted the broken-window principle. The broken-window principle is that if you don't fix broken windows or whatever else shows decay, then the neighborhood does not take care of its community. People come to expect things to be run-down and broken. But if you fix the broken windows, people see that you care about their surroundings, and everyone puts more effort into keeping the community safe and clean. Using this principle, Guiliani cleaned up Time Square and other run-down areas and saw a dramatic decrease in crime.

By setting the tone for what is respectful and safe behavior for the school (and for the home) and enforcing those standards, a school can improve its social health and get everyone working together to create an open and safe environment for learning.

That is the lesson learned at San Marcos High School in California. A "hit list" was discovered where one child identified all of his tormentors and marked them for being killed. The parents of some of the kids on the list wanted the school to do something about it. So Principal Frans Weits ordered an investigation, then took action against those involved in the incident, including the students whose behavior landed them on that list. "In light of what's happened at neighboring districts, San Marcos High now has a zero-tolerance policy toward bullying," Weits told *The San Diego Union Tribune*.[2] Students and staff got the message: "Students will be held accountable for everything from verbal harassment to physical aggression." Suddenly more reports of bullying started to surface, and more investigations were launched. Kids felt that the school was safer and that their reporting would be taken seriously.

Setting high standards for respectful words and behavior in school can become the norm and thus self-perpetuating. Principals, counselors, social workers, and teachers can make a huge difference in setting a respectful tone in a school. Whether kids talking to adults helps or not depends almost entirely on how the adults handle the information and if they respond in a thoughtful and conscientious manner.

The goal is to create a climate of respect that dignifies both students and those in authority and encourages everyone to get involved. In this chapter we will explore ways that parents and educators can encourage just such an atmosphere.

WHAT PARENTS CAN DO

Here are some general tips for parents for how to work with schools about bullying.

- *Communicate with the school.* Parent-school communication is vital for addressing bullying situations. Start with the teacher or staff member most directly involved. Often students and parents assume teachers know about incidents when that is not necessarily so. If further help is needed, or if the teacher is hesitant to help, call the school social worker, counselor, dean, or principal.

- *Give the school the benefit of the doubt.* Begin by assuming they are interested in helping solve the problem along with you. A staff person may at first try to minimize the situation so as not to add to their already busy day. Usually a firm assurance that you are taking the bullying seriously will get them to take you seriously.

- *Develop a strategy for your call or meeting.* Have accurate information; ask your child all the details about the incidents, including where they have occurred, how often, when they started, and your child's responses to the bullying. Be open to looking at your child's behavior and how it may be contributing to the bully situation.

- *Bring a written summary of the incidents.* Also take notes on what plan you and the school develop for dealing with the situation, especially with regard to the specific responsibilities of the teacher, parent, and administrator.

- *Join with the administrator to adjust schedules, seating, and/or locker assignment to limit access between the bully and your child.* This strategy only works for passive victims who do not initiate any verbal or physical contact with the bully, but it can be a relatively simple way to make dramatic improvements in a victim's life. It is a case of removing the opportunity and thus removing the bullying.

- *Request that additional supervision and/or monitoring be provided in the target bully areas* (hallways during passing periods, locker rooms, bathrooms, playgrounds, lunchrooms) where supervision is reduced.

- *Follow up with school personnel about progress and difficulties with the situation.* Often schools do not hear back from parents when things are going better.

WHAT EDUCATORS CAN DO

Just like parents, teachers can make a big difference in either reducing or exacerbating a bullying problem. Lindsey, a high school junior, reports, "I had a friend who was getting picked on by a clique leader—mostly calling her names like 'slut.' She was really upset and went to a teacher to try to get help. It made everything worse. They just ignored it. The girl kept picking on her until there was a physical fight and both got suspensions. My friend's parents were mad at the teachers and counselors for ignoring it. Ignoring it just made it bigger." Ignoring a kid's legitimate cry for help breeds feelings of helplessness, despair, and cynicism in kids.

On the other hand, teachers can make all the difference in making a bullied kid's life much better. One junior, Sarah, described how her teacher Mrs. Jennings saved her when she was in seventh grade. Sarah was new to the school and was getting picked on by some other girls. She was overweight, wore glasses, and had braces. The clique saw her as a target. Most of the verbal abuse was happening at lunch. Mrs. Jennings noticed some exchanges in the hallway and told Sarah that she always ate lunch in her classroom, so if Sarah wanted to come in and eat and be an office aid for her she could. Sarah was saved! Mrs. Jennings' sensitivity not only got her away from the bullies, but it also gave her some responsibility that built her self-esteem. Sarah said, "I'll always remember what she told me, 'Hang in there. It won't always be like this.' And she was right. Those were dark days in my life, but now I have friends, and I don't give a rip what girls like that think about anything!"

According to school social worker Pam Greenagel, L.C.S.W., simply taking the time to intervene on the smaller incidents of bullying helps prevent bullying from getting out of hand. "It is important to find out when the bullying is happening, what has already been tried by the student, and address it as administrators when the behavior is continuing. Nine times out of ten a talk from the dean stops the bullying. We run a pretty tight ship."

Here are some tips for administrators and teachers for what parents are looking for regarding bullying problems.

- *Communicate to parents and students a clear anti-bullying policy.* Since Columbine and the rash of school shootings, many school districts have adopted tough anti-bullying policies. The problem usually isn't that there is not a policy in place, but that it is not being communicated and consistently followed. (One aspect of those plans that many are now questioning is what is meant by "zero tolerance." It usually means that once a child performs an act that the administration determines to be bullying, the consequence is automatic and severe, usually beginning with suspension. Many administrators want to make sure that they retain some flexibility when administering the consequence to the bully. According to Mark McDonald, a deputy superintendent in the Chicago area, "You don't want to get a boy expelled for a year because he and a friend were play acting." Instead, he recommends that schools adopt a bullying policy that allows the administrator to consider each case on its own merit. At the same time, zero-tolerance policies can create liability problems if the same punishment is not meted out every time while the written policy says it should be. The goal is to create a clear expectation that there will be strong consequences to bullying behavior.)

- *Listen and summarize a parent's concerns.* Although time may be critically short, it is still important to take time to hear the concern and let the parents know they have been heard. Bullying is potentially a very serious safety concern. A small investment of time and attention at the beginning of the problem may save lives, reduce harm, and prevent an even larger investment of energies later.

- *Inform parents of their options.* Often parents feel insecure and confused when dealing with schools, because they don't have any idea what options are available to solve the problem. Their lack of knowledge can create feelings of vulnerability.

- *Be patient.* Parents may feel they have to protect their child, but they don't know what that means at this point. For many people, even going to the school can push them way beyond their comfort zones. They might come across as more belligerent and aggressive than is needed because they are working themselves up to confront the problem. They can come across like a rebel without a cause—lots of fight and not enough focus. If the parents become adversarial, don't respond in kind. Assure them that everyone wants what is best for their son or daughter and develop a plan that addresses their concerns.

- *Intervene.* Often minor structural changes, such as changes in scheduling or seat assignment or increased supervision in locker rooms, bathrooms, buses, and playgrounds, can take little effort for an educator and yet have a profound impact on a child's life. Also, taking the time to intervene when you witness minor incidents of kids being cruel to other kids sends a clear message that it will not be tolerated.

- *Develop an anonymous means by which students and parents can inform the school about bullying incidents.* Once this system is seen as secure, the information garnered will increase. One school principal tells a story about how taking the time to get to the reasons for the behaviors can provide a key to turning the situation around: "We got a new student transfer into eighth grade, an African-American girl, who started to bully and harass an African-American boy who went to the school. He had a physical disability, was adopted by a white family, and so he didn't speak the Black vernacular. The girl called him an 'oreo' and said he acted 'white.' He was deeply offended. Soon all his African-American friends befriended the girl, and he became isolated in the mostly white school. She told everyone that he spoke as if he were gay. We had several sessions with the parents and the kids. We discovered that one of the reasons the boy got picked on was because he would lash back at the girl with vulgar language. We also found that one of the reasons he was upset was because he felt he was losing all his friends to this girl. After several sessions, we learned that the boy's father had abandoned him and that his name had been changed. The girl opened up about sexual abuse. She hadn't realized that the boy felt threatened by the loss of friends. They discovered that they had a lot in common. Now they stick together. When someone else called him a vulgar name, the former bully stuck up for him."

- *Follow up.* Give parents updates on the progress of the problem until it is resolved. Return their phone calls when they are trying to follow up with you.

Mary tells of her frustration from working with fellow parents in order to solve a bullying problem. She only saw progress when she asked the school to make some changes. "In sixth grade John was involved with a group of boys, led by Mitch and Brian, who had absolutely no regard for anyone who was not an athlete. They decided among themselves who was 'in' and who was 'out.' Well, Mitch and Brian decided that John was a 'wimp' and he was out, mostly because he was one of the few boys who would talk to girls as friends. Others followed Mitch and Brian's example and excluded John from playground games or made sure he suffered if he did play. They pushed him and told him to go swing with the girls.

"Unfortunately, their main teacher was distracted that year because he was going through a divorce, and so he allowed some of the bullying dynamics into the classroom. I got tired of hearing the same stories from John every day and seeing him suffer. Since Mitch was a neighbor and involved with the same soccer team, I decided to have his parents over to talk about the problem. I warned them ahead of time what we would talk about. The conversation was very difficult. The husband was concerned about Mitch's behavior but the mom was not. She told me, 'Now, Mary, you have to remember that these are boys, and they are going to do this to each other.'

"That cut me like a knife, as a mother and as a friend. I had taken a risk with a friend of mine, and they were unwilling to work with their son to change. I had to end the friendship after that.

"Finally, I met with the teacher, and we decided to separate Mitch and Brian's desks as much as possible. This helped but did not solve the problem of group time. Next I went to the principal and said it would really be helpful if these two kids were not in the same classes in seventh grade, and he listened to it. That pretty much took care of the problem."

WHAT PARENTS SHOULD NOT DO

Just as parents can interact with schools in effective ways, the approach they take can also jeopardize the outcome of the situation for their kids. Here are some additional suggestions for parents, much of it gathered from interviews with teachers and school administrators.

- *Don't become defensive with administrators.* Take the time to calm yourself and your spouse (if needed) before you call or meet with the school. A calm, rational approach engenders both credibility and cooperation. Be open to feedback about your child's behavior as well.

- *Avoid all-or-nothing thinking and language.* It is natural to imagine the bullying child as evil personified or your child as angelically pure. If the educators resist this framework for understanding the situation, you may feel your hands start to sweat, your heart speed up, and your voice rise in volume. But bullying the school through power and intimidation does not solve the problem and provides a negative example for your child of how one is supposed to solve problems. Threatening a law suit shuts down communication in a big way.

- *Don't interrupt.* Hear the teacher out about her understanding of the situation and her plan to solve the problem. Educators often have a more holistic understanding of the situation. What you at first object to might be explained later.

WHAT EDUCATORS SHOULD NOT DO

- *Don't become defensive*. Parents may need to blow off steam about the situation. Don't take it personally. Verbally validate their concerns, then redirect and refocus the conversation toward developing a solution. For example, saying, "I can understand completely why you are so upset. I think it is best that we move into developing a plan together to deal with the situation," can diffuse the situation and redirect the energy.
- *Don't use complex and confusing language or professional jargon*. In other words, simplify your language. In many areas, teachers average much more education than the average parent in their district. Parents are mindful of this gap, and when they hear jargon and professional terms, they will hear it as condescending, which will make them defensive and reinforce their sense of vulnerability. I have my doctorate and consider myself a fairly educated individual. Yet I have been surprised at how many times I have not been able to follow all the jargon used during parent-teacher conferences.

The ideal is to create an environment in the school and community where bullying is unacceptable. This can happen with just a few people taking the lead, whether administrators or students.

WHEN TO CHANGE SCHOOLS

One school social worker tells the story of getting a transfer student whom they were worried about. In his former junior high, the boy was getting into twelve to fourteen verbal fights a day with students and six times a day with adults. But in the new school he seemed to have no problems. Finally, the social worker met with the student and explained her puzzlement: "The kid we saw on paper before you came, and the kid we see here now are not the same. What's the difference?" The boy answered, "Nobody starts with me here, and no one messes with me here." He is now on the wrestling team. The social worker arranged babysitting for his younger brother so he didn't have to watch him. The boy's life has been transformed.

Changing schools can work. It can turn a bullying situation around. But it should never be undertaken lightly. Here are some criteria that can help you make that choice.

1. *The school administration won't listen.* One set of parents reported that in response to their concern that a bullying situation would not be addressed, the principal said, "If you leave the school, it will be one less set of parents I have to deal with!" This sort of disrespect starts at the top and works down to the students.

2. *Bullying is the dominant culture in the school.* If the school has allowed physical and emotional intimidation to become entrenched in the school social system, then it is unrealistic for one or even a few families to overturn the system in a short time.

3. *The problem is chronic and has extended an entire school year or more.* Being the victim of bullies is extremely draining for your child and significantly affects his or her school performance. You do not want your child to fall into a hole that he or she will have difficulty climbing out of.

4. *The child is depressed.*

5. *The child has exercised several assertive strategies without significant results.*

6. *You feel a strong leading to make a change and have researched other options.*

In considering a new school for your child, make sure you determine it has a solid antibullying policy and, if it does, how well it works. If you are told, "We don't have that problem here," don't believe it. The problem exists in all schools.

School bullying is everyone's business. It is unrealistic to expect it can be eliminated. We can't eradicate the conditions that turn some children into bullies and others into targets.

But if everyone concerned—teachers, school authorities, police, parents, and children—is truly committed to not tolerating bullying, then the amount and the severity of bullying can be reduced dramatically.

Chapter Seven
School Intervention and Prevention Programs

A teacher affects eternity;
he can never tell where his influence stops.

— HENRY ADAMS

Schools vary considerably on what interventions, if any, are being pursued to combat bullying. The range extends from a strictly punitive approach, where the principal doles out suspensions and detentions, to a thoroughly integrated program of respect and character development that affects almost every aspect of school life.

While there is not one antibullying model that can be applied to all schools, the best programs share some of the same attributes: multifaceted, multileveled (involving staff, students, and parents), ongoing, with data-driven evaluation. The focus of these programs is ambitious and broad but concentrates on respect, character, and choices.

The impact of successful programs is pervasive. The qualities of responsibility and cooperation permeate the school culture, both in the classroom and in other social activities. Developing a respectful school culture is a challenging task in an era of diversity and mainstreaming and with the complex demands placed on schools for national testing and statewide requirements.

Some schools are pursuing respect and seeing significant results every moment in their schools. A wide range of resources are available through books, programs, and the Internet. Many resources and services are local, serving schools in their areas. A sampling of some of the best resources will be reviewed in this chapter and in more depth in Appendix A, with Web sites and contact information noted. You may want to work through area school districts to discover the best local programs available.

Another common attribute of successful programs is that they are hard to pull off. In story after story, I found the success was due to one person—a teacher, principal, parent, or student—who saw the bullying problem in the school and decided to do something about it. In all cases the individual met with resistance, from staff who "just want to teach math" to kids who say fatalistically, "It's just the way it is around here." As John Seaman Garnes once said, "Real leaders are ordinary people with extraordinary determinations."

Comprehensive programs can make the critical difference in the school lives of our children. Psychologist Dan Olweus of Norway developed a systematic school-based bullying intervention program in response to the 1982 suicide of three Norwegian boys, ages ten through fourteen, apparently as a result of severe bullying by their classmates. Within two years of the program's implementation, the incidents of school bullying had dropped by more than 50 percent. A number of countries, including England, Germany, and the United States, have implemented Olweus's program with similar results.

The choice of whether a school deals with bullying or not is of vital significance to our children. It can make the difference between success and failure in life as well as in school. As we have seen, the wounds from bullying can run deep, and the consequences last a lifetime.

The hardest part of dealing with bullying, like any problem in our culture today, is time. It is extremely difficult to take the time necessary for planning, learning, researching, consulting, evaluating, implementing, and following up changes to a school culture. Yet, taking this time may be one of the best investments our schools make in our children. Preventive medicine is almost always less expensive in the long run than treating the disease itself. In the same way, if we can prevent the soul wounds that come from bullying, we will have freed many people to live healthier, more fulfilling lives, and we will have created better citizens and better communities.

Next we will review programs on peer mediation, respect and character, conflict resolution, comprehensive bully strategies, and antibullying theater. A full list of resources with descriptions is contained in Appendix A. The multifaceted nature of bullying requires interventions that build a variety of skills into the student body.

PEER MEDIATION PROGRAMS

The goal of peer mediation is to train students—usually those who are identified by staff as older and more mature—to resolve disputes involving other students. They have been around long enough to be studied thoroughly and have proven to be an effective means of resolving disputes. According to one summary of the data, "Success rates of 58 percent to 93 percent have been achieved at various sites where success was measured by whether an agreement was reached and maintained at the time of a follow-up evaluation."[1]

There are many reasons the range is so wide on effectiveness. For example, one school social worker who headed up the peer mediation program at her school for seven years just stopped it. She reported that it was too time-consuming to train the kids, that certain kids were not effective, and that streamlining the discipline to the principal was more efficient. The main variables to control for effectiveness appear to be student selection, districtwide involvement (as opposed to only one school), and adult oversight of the formal mediation sessions. Statistically tracking the incidences of bullying in a school is essential to judging the effectiveness of these programs. In addition, it is often the climate of the school that is affected by peer mediators, and this may be subtle and difficult to measure.

Not only has peer mediation been found to be effective, but the students who get the training also have an added benefit. They are able to apply their training in nonviolent conflict resolution to other areas of their lives. "Students have reported using their mediation skills to resolve disputes at home with their siblings and in their community with peers. Students who are taught the skills of mediating disputes learn political skills, which can be used beyond the classroom. Student mediators learn to listen effectively, summarize accurately, and think critically. Further, they develop skills on how to solve problems, to lead, to write, and to foster meaningful discussion among disputants. Since mediation seeks to solve a dispute and prevent its recurrence, student mediators learn to plan for the future. They learn about responsibilities as well as rights, about consequences as well as choices."[2]

Not only do the mediators learn important life skills, but often so do the disputants. "Maybe for the first time in their lives, they learn nonviolent ways that they can choose to resolve their conflicts. They learn that they can succeed at resolving conflicts peaceably, that they can resolve problems without resorting to violence. They also develop a capacity to empathize with others."[3]

Here is how it works. Mediators often work in areas where there is traditionally little adult oversight, such as on the playground or in the lunchroom. Mediators may work alone or in groups. When they see a pair in conflict, they may immediately intervene, inviting the participants to try to work out their problems with the mediator's help. If they agree, the process begins. First, everyone moves to a safe area where the group can talk freely and privately. If the students involved in the conflict don't want to participate, the mediators do nothing. They are not the same as a student police force.

In mediating among older students, cases are more often referred to them. Often an adult is present to supervise the sessions, which some educators believe is essential for it to work. Anonymity is one key to the success of a program.[4] "Anonymous means of reporting problems to school officials, through mediators, guidance counselors, teachers, and students has been a hallmark of most successful programs. Some outstanding programs forbid the person who received the report from sharing the name of the 'informant' with anyone, including the principal. This policy secures confidentiality and ultimately the integrity of the entire anonymous reporting structure."

The majority of mediation programs take place in middle schools with some systems providing high school mediators to their middle school kids.

Mary Wade-Hicks is the Student Assistance Program Coordinator at a suburban school. Wade-Hicks started peer mediation in her district ten years ago on her own initiative.

Since then her role has expanded districtwide. She has tracked a steady decrease, approximately 10 percent per year, of violent crimes in the district.

She combined the material by Fred Schrumpf entitled *Peer Mediation* (see Appendix A) with some other conflict resolution manuals. She also adjusted timetables so the student mediators could be trained in a condensed format during one school day.

According to Wade-Hicks, the key to a successful peer mediation program is the selection of student mediators. She starts with teacher recommendations. "We are looking for kids who may have some clout with their peers, are without a record of trouble, have resiliency, and demonstrate participation in the community." Other educators suggest that potential mediators be screened through brief, one-on-one interviews.

Once the kids are accepted and parental permission is secured, they are invited to a training day. After the training day, the kids who would be the best mediators are assigned. Kids perceive it as an honor and a chance to exercise leadership. Kids who don't have the top skills get assigned other jobs, observe longer, or train some more for later in the year.

Wade-Hicks also has a peer mentor program where older kids work with younger ones. Each mentor is trained in character education and in certain exercises-decision-dilemma situations, role-taking, listening skills, manners, tolerance, empathy, and respect. She has one hundred ten students at the high school involved in the program. The high school mentors are bused every day to elementary and middle schools. Each mentor is assigned either to a classroom or to individuals at lunch time. They can work on academics, relationship building, or character building. Their influence is truly a "successful blend of the academic and social aspects of school. They take the edge off the issues."

RESPECT AND CHARACTER PROGRAMS

"Character development is the great, if not the sole, aim of education," said William O'Shea. There are numerous character curricula for all types of schools. Sorting through them all can be confusing, so take a close look at Appendix A.

One of these programs, *Character Counts*, has received mixed reviews among school administrators. Many administrators state that the design of the program is best suited to elementary school students. Some schools describe the curriculum as a "rah rah" program, with a great deal of enthusiasm but not enough substance and depth. Other schools have used it as a base program and have supplemented it with other programs and teacher ideas. *Character Counts'* most significant achievement is in getting a serious values curriculum back into the public schools.

Shirley LeClere, the principal of Smith Elementary School in Aurora, Illinois, took the ideas from various character programs and developed her own homegrown version. The results have been impressive. LeClere now gives workshops to other schools to teach the program she has developed over the last several years.

Smith Elementary School has a challenging mixture of students. In addition to overcrowding, 60 percent of the student body come from low-income backgrounds and live in government-subsidized housing projects. The other 40 percent are blue-collar, lower-middle-class families. The racial mix of the school is 38 percent African-American, 38 percent Hispanic, and 24 percent Caucasian.

She calls her program "The 7 Habits of Highly Effective Students," because she loosely based the program on some of the principles in Stephen Covey's book, *Seven Habits of Highly*

Effective People. Over the several years of the program she has documented an improvement in the discipline statistics, the school culture, and in the school's performance on statewide standardized tests. In addition, she has garnered more parent and community support than she had before the program was implemented. By December 1, 2001, she had not seen a single discipline problem in her office for that academic year. Although many problems had occurred in the school, they had been addressed through the program.

LeClere set out to teach a culture both to teachers and to students. "Respect" is broken down into habits like being on time for class, showing effort, not bullying, and a myriad of other behaviors. The seven core habits she identified through meetings with teachers, parents, and students are responsibility, perseverance, honesty, cooperation, respect, pride, and courtesy. The longer list of habits was developed by taking the core habits and the school's existing rules and developing a list of proactive and positive behaviors that extend from the core values.

First, she created a pamphlet-sized guide for the classroom teachers to use in weekly family meetings with their students. The pamphlet reviews each of the habits, defines them with examples and elaborates on their importance in school. A local business group had given the school a grant to train teachers in a respect program. LeClere sent seven teachers for two weeks of full-time, paid training in the summer. These teachers became the trainers for the remainder of the staff. Their training included problem-solving, conflict resolution, respectful communication, win-win negotiation, character building, and using "I" messages.

The seven habits are integrated into the classroom, playground, and everywhere on the campus. The school T-shirts have them emblazoned on them. Posters of the seven habits go home with every child and have become a supplemental parenting tool. Each classroom regularly receives one literary hardback book on the Habit of the Month, which is reviewed and discussed during the class meetings. For the class meeting, the teacher is the facilitator. When a new teacher is learning the process, a counselor, social worker, or the principal might sit in to help out.

They use a Problem Bag to collect problems all week. At the class meetings all problems are pulled out of the bag, and each is reviewed. The Problem Bag is a brown paper bag posted in the classroom where kids can write issues down anonymously. Solutions and options are developed as a group. This process gives kids ownership of their problems and of their solutions. Kids can also write down something they tried that worked well to share with others. The class meeting also focuses on the positive achievements of the class. In this environment kids feel comfortable and safe.

The curriculum is tied to everything at school. When a historical or literary character is discussed, the children are asked to examine the person's character and identify which of the seven habits are present and how they are seen. Once a month, students can be nominated for the Pride Board. Students and teachers state what a student did, which habit was expressed, and how it was exemplified to win the monthly award.

In addition, each teacher has a Behavioral Support Partner. This is a separate teacher in a separate classroom where kids go for time-out. So, rather than taking a time-out in her own classroom, the student goes elsewhere to cool off. If she is still acting out, then a behavioral contract is written. It is a typical contract with problem identification, choices or options, and preferred alternative actions. When it is completed, it is circled and signed off by the student and the teacher. Very few of these contracts are broken. If behavior continues to escalate, then a teacher-parent behavioral contract meeting is held. Both agree to follow up. If this fails, then the principal meets with the parents and child to develop further contracts and interventions or to invoke a suspension.

CONFLICT RESOLUTION

I Can Problem Solve (ICPS) is a conflict resolution program for schools. Through the program, impulsive students become more social, better able to cope with frustration, and more patient. Inhibited youngsters become more outgoing and better able to stand up for their rights. ICPS is available for three developmental levels: preschool, kindergarten and primary grades, and intermediate elementary grades. It has been field-tested extensively in schools across the country. The curriculum involves formal lessons, interaction in the classroom, and integration into the regular school curriculum. The program teaches social awareness skills, empathy, option generating, and personal impact.

One suburban middle school principal and assistant principal decided to target character education and conflict resolution as the basis for their school culture. Five years prior, the school pursued one of the standard character education programs for the students. The key character traits they identified were respect, responsibility, self-discipline, positive attitude, kindness, honesty, trust, and integrity. This list of values was developed from PTA meetings and faculty meetings, so the outcome had shared ownership. These values are posted outside the school.

Next Dennis Rosy, the principal of Franklin Middle School in Wheaton, Illinois, decided to be radical. He realized that the staff were in need of a communication transformation as well as character training. After some didactic training in "I" language and conflict resolution skills, he hired an outside consultant to come in for four days of communication training (two hours each day). He targeted a year for the staff to get "up to speed" and then to address the kids' programs.

He noticed some dramatic changes in the teachers' abilities to talk with each other directly without fear of hurting each other's feelings. The staff now integrates the character traits into literary and historical studies, field trips, and every other aspect of school. Being late for class is not just being tardy; it is marked off and discussed for its impact on others. "How does it affect your classmates when you are late? Being on time shows respect for everyone's learning time."

Modeling respect in disciplinary situations is especially challenging and important. "Kids view respect as conditional, and if it is not reciprocated, they know it. We have to model that respect, even when it's overwhelming. I even tell kids that sometimes the kids have to model respect for the grownups," says Rosy. He has found that a Socratic style of questioning (versus lecturing) is more effective and gets the kids more involved.

The Character Education Committee consists of parents and students from each grade level. They plan several activities a year and meet once a month. For example, the committee planned an antidrug fundraiser and gave the money to a local orphanage for cocaine babies. They sponsored a Loose Change campaign for September 11th families and raised $1,000. They are relaunching a peer mediation program in 2002, which was dropped a few years back. The school recently hosted Bridge-work Theater (see Appendix A) to present *Krista's Enemy*, a play that focuses on conflict resolution and the impact of bystanders.

Bullying situations are divided between the guidance counselor and the team leader. Guidance counselors follow their class through the three years of middle school for continuity. Kids are asked, "What would you like to do to set this right?" They can write essays or apologize. All kids are asked to identify which of the eight traits was affected by their negative behavior. Assistant Principal Dan Sullivan says, "We ask kids if they can apologize from the heart and mean it; otherwise your integrity doesn't mean anything. Similarly, saying 'sorry' means that you won't repeat the negative behavior; otherwise you are jeopardizing your integrity. Even when the child is getting a suspension, we want to maintain his dignity."

All of this conflict resolution takes a great deal of time. Principal Rosy tells kids that the negative habit will continue in their lives if they don't address it. "When parents don't respond to a kid in trouble for bullying, the worst part is that the kid knows that the parent doesn't care enough to come to school or return my calls. We want to involve the parents." Some strategies include asking the parent to come into the cafeteria and sit unannounced. "It is so powerful. The kid knows the parent cares and so do other kids. Sometimes kids back off just seeing that."

Parents are also encouraged to come to school to check their child's locker. Some kids, who are bullies, write nasty things about other kids in a notebook called a SLAM book. They are making fun of other kids when their teachers are not looking and then passing it around to friends. Reading through a confiscated SLAM book can help the parent better understand a child's participation in bullying.

Even this optimistic administrative team did have to acknowledge that getting parents of bullies involved in solving the problem is often difficult. The parents are often uninvolved with the kids and often refuse to become so.

One last bit of advice from Rosy is that teasing is inevitable for the middle-school age group. "Developmentally the child is looking for power and where she stands. We suggest that the kids look at how deep the friendship is. How deep your friendship is determines the amount you can tease a person. We want the kids to begin to understand their audience. If you are not close to a person, the receiver of the teasing will not perceive it as teasing or fun."

BULLY PROGRAMS

These programs focus on increasing awareness of bullying, increasing teacher and parent supervision, establishing clear rules to prohibiting bullying, and providing support and protection for those who are being bullied. Two multifaceted programs are reviewed in Appendix A.

Bully programs suggest interventions at the classroom level. For example, Dan Olweus, a foremost expert on bullying, has developed a program that he recounts in his book *Bullying at School*. Olweus recommends using a curriculum that promotes kindness, communication, cooperation, friendship, empathy, anger management, and conflict resolution skills. This curriculum should have a role-playing component that includes acting out nonaggressive behavior with bullies and the role-playing of assertive behavior with victims. Next he suggests developing some brief but clear class rules against bullying. An example of classroom rules are "(1) We will not bully other students, (2) We will try to help students who are bullied, (3) We will include students who might be left out."[5] Many educators agree that empathy training is one of the key components in trying to reform a bully.

One eighth grade science teacher reported, "Our school is

really weak on bullying. We don't have any programs. Right now any kids caught bullying just go see the principal. It doesn't help; the behavior doesn't change. I was so concerned about it myself I went to the Don't Laugh at Me workshop on my own time and at my own expense. It is a curriculum that addresses respect on several levels. I advocated that our school adopt it. We are going ahead with it in the spring semester." One teacher's heart is making a big impact on a system and its children.

THEATER PROGRAMS

Some argue that theater can have the most profound impact on children's attitudes because it comes in through the back door. Many, if not most, school administrators agree that it can be a tremendous complement to a multifaceted antibullying program. Because of the nature of theater, most groups serve a limited area.

Don Yost is the director and playwright of Bridgeworks, a theater group that tours the schools of the Midwest, presenting plays on problems kids face, such as bullying. It takes a year to develop a new play. Yost starts by surverying teachers, therapists, administrators, parents, and students to develop a list of problems that can be addressed in theater. After topics are picked he goes back and researches the particular issue and what programs exist for the problem. He then talks with several groups of kids in groups of three or four to see what their perceptions are about what will work. During this process he often hears real stories from kids that are incorporated into the play. After the script is written, it is read for groups of children to obtain their feedback for changes. Then the play is produced and evaluated for its effectiveness for attitude change with a control group. Inevitably it is revised again. The authenticity of the play is integral to its success.

There is a school packet with teacher training materials that goes along with each play. It is a limited but useful curriculum that is set up with pre- and post-play activities. The play concepts are built around the life of the classroom as are the materials. According to Yost, "Theater is a powerful way to change attitudes, but it is a one-time event, and most bullying requires ongoing interventions." Yost has advice to parents and teachers: "Teachers influence children whether they know it or not. They are being watched very closely and carefully. The people inside a school make a huge difference. Teachers are the real heroes."

He also cautions parents to remember that middle school students today are much more sophisticated about bullying than we think they are. He has found that they have a variety of ways of handling bullying situations that they have already tried before they come to an adult to talk about it.

Not all plays have to be professionally produced to be helpful in fighting bullying. Diane is a senior in high school, who wrote a play for a seminar class. She is a leader in her school, who is actively involved with both her school's antidrug campaign and also in her school's gay/straight alliance group. Her goal was for people to notice that joking by saying things like "that's so gay" can be very hurtful, even though it may seem small at the time. Her play was performed twice at the school, and the feedback from students was outstanding. She portrayed six high school students—the drug dude, the gay guy, the perfect student, the cutter and suicidal girl, the Goth kid, and the bully. The point of the play was that even though these students looked vastly different from the outside, they had the same needs, concerns, and feelings on the inside. I asked some students what programs had helped with respect and bullying, and one replied, "The student-directed play had a big impact on me. There were six people, and the play really talked about how they treated and felt about each other. It had a big effect in our school." Encouraging student leaders to be creative and involved can have a profound impact on a school culture.

The Difference You Can Make

What can you do about bullying? Quite a lot. The home and school environments shape a child's world and future. Taking time to implement some of the effective strategies in this book—whether at home, at school, or at your church—can turn the lives of many children around. Bullying can have devastating consequences for its victims and for those who witness the bullying. And research has proven that, if adults pay attention to the problem and develop a strategy for dealing with it, incidences of bullying can be greatly reduced and the consequences minimized.

Not only are bullying programs worthwhile because they are effective, they have other benefits as well. Teaching parents, teachers, and students respectful communication improves the quality of life for an entire community. Who would not benefit from learning assertive and effective communication styles or from modeling them for kids? So encourage your school through PTA or by another means to set up a capable and comprehensive respect program. Tap into the resources in the Appendices to get the ball rolling in your area. This is an important way to serve as salt and light in the challenging and intimidating world around us. One person can make the difference, and that person just might be you.

Appendix A
Resources for Schools and Parents

PEER MEDIATION PROGRAMS

Fred Schrumpf. *Peer Mediation: Conflict Resolution in Schools: Program Guide*. Research Press, 1997.

Fred Schrumpf, D. Crawford, and H. Usadel. *Peer Mediation: Conflict Resolution in Schools*. Research Press, 1997.

Schrumpf's book and its program come highly recommended from a variety of school social workers who have implemented the concepts. They report a high degree of success. The peer mediation program can be adapted to elementary, middle, or high schools.

RESPECT AND CHARACTER PROGRAMS

Character Counts
Josephson Institute of Ethics
Attn: Character Development Seminars

4640 Admiralty Way, Suite 1001
Marina del Rey, CA 90292-6610
(800) 711-2670
www.charactercounts.org
For K through 12

Character Counts is a nonpartisan, nonsectarian coalition of schools, communities, and nonprofit organizations working to advance character education by teaching the Six Pillars of Character: trustworthiness, respect, responsibility, fairness, caring, and citizenship. The coalition works to overcome the false but surprisingly powerful notions that no single value is intrinsically superior to another; that ethical values vary by race, class, gender, and politics; that greed and fairness, cheating and honesty carry the same moral weight, simply depending on one's perspective and immediate needs. Effective character education does not dismiss the importance of self-esteem but maintains that ethical values must be ranked above expedience and personal preference. Character education sets up objective criteria of virtue and encourages young people to adopt them as ground rules for life.

Character Development Seminars (CDS) are the coalition's primary means of training and certifying teachers, community leaders, coaches, and other leaders of youth organizations to teach principled reasoning and ethical decision making based on the Six Pillars of Character. They also offer products and publications, many of which are free. Their Web site has information and curriculum ideas from its members in the coalition.

Right Choices
Worldview Publishing
521 Herchel Drive

Tampa, FL 33617
(800) 987-9444

Right Choices is a conflict resolution, social skills, and discipline program for teenagers. It calls itself a "simple to use, video-driven, social skills, conflict resolution training program" that promises to reduce referrals for conflicts and aggression by 50 percent. It can be used either in a single classroom or a whole school. Its goal is violence prevention and character building by letting students practice taking responsibility for their choices on a daily basis. They use a five-step model that breaks down a student's choices:

(1) "I need to think about this."
(2) "What kind of choice do I want to make—good or bad?"
(3) "What are my choices and consequences?"
(4) "I need to pick one choice and do it."
(5) "How did I do?"

In the end, the program seeks to build up eight skill areas: problem solving, apologizing, negotiating, using self-control, standing up for your rights, responding to teasing, keeping out of fights, and dealing with peer pressure.

CONFLICT RESOLUTION

I Can Problem-Solve: An Interpersonal Cognitive Problem-Solving (ICPS) Intervention
Preschool, Kindergarten and Primary Grades, and
Intermediate Elementary Grades
For program information, contact,
Dr. Myrna B. Shure
Research Press

245 N. 15th St.
MS 626
Philadelphia, PA 19102
(215) 762-7205

I Can Problem Solve (ICPS) serves as an effective violence prevention program by helping children think of nonviolent ways to solve everyday problems. ICPS is a cognitive approach that teaches children *how* to think, rather than telling them *what* to think. They learn that behavior has causes, that people have feelings, and that there is more than one way to solve a problem. As they learn to associate how they think with what they do, children become more caring and better able to share, cooperate, and get along with others.

BULLY PROGRAMS

Bullying at School: What We Know and What We Can Do
Dan Olweus
Blackwell, 1993

Olweus is the premier international expert on bullying. He has developed measures that he considers to be critical to the effectiveness of any antibullying program. He also describes the components of the program in Norway that reduced incidences of bullying dramatically:
- Awareness and involvement on the part of adults, with regard to bully/victim problems
- A survey of bully/victim problems at the start of the intervention
- A school conference day devoted to bully/victim problems

- Better supervision during recess and lunch hour by adults (also bathrooms, hallways, etc.)
- Consistent and immediate consequences for aggressive behavior
- Generous praise for prosocial and helpful behavior by students
- Specific class rules against bullying
- Class meetings about bullying
- Serious individual talks with bullies and with victims
- Serious talks with parents of bullies and victims
- A meeting of the PTA on school bullying
- Student representatives to evaluate the program's success[1]

Don't Laugh at Me (DLAM) Program

Elementary (Grades 2–5) and Middle School (Grades 6–8)
Operation Respect
2 Penn Plaza, 23rd Floor
New York, NY 10121
www.don'tlaugh.org

The Don't Laugh at Me Project (DLAM) is working to transform schools, camps, and other youth organizations into more compassionate, safe, and respectful environments for children. Founded by Peter Yarrow of the folk group Peter, Paul & Mary, the project disseminates educational resources that are designed to establish a climate that reduces the emotional and physical cruelty some children inflict upon each other by behaviors such as ridicule, bullying and, in extreme cases, violence. DLAM has developed three curricula, one for grades 2–5, another for grades 6–8, and a third for summer camps and after-school programs. All utilize inspiring music and video, as well as materials based on the well-tested, highly regarded conflict resolution curricula developed by the Resolving Conflict Creatively Program of Educators for Social Responsibility. DLAM is a gateway program; it is designed to provide teachers, school counselors, social workers, administrators, and other professionals with an entry point for year-round social and emotional learning and character education programs.

Through music, video, and classroom activities, the DLAM program helps sensitize children to the painful effects of behaviors that too often are accepted as necessary rites of passage in childhood—ridicule, disrespect (or "dissing"), ostracism, and bullying. This program is designed to inspire children, along with their teachers and other educators, to transform their classrooms and schools into "Ridicule-Free Zones." Students and educators then take mutual responsibility for preserving the climate they have created.

THEATER PROGRAMS

Bridgework Theater
  113 1/2 E. Lincoln Avenue
  Goshen, IN 46528-3228
  (800) 200-1602
  Email: info@bridgework.org
  www.bridgework.org

Bridgework Theater presents violence-prevention plays for over 150,000 children each year. Founded in 1979, the theater has programs for children on anger management, conflict resolution, and teasing and bullying. Their plays address real-life problems of young people and model proven methods that

empower youth to develop nonviolent solutions to those problems. The plays *entertain* as well as *educate*. They promise that
even the most distracted students (the ones who need help the
most) pay attention because: 1) They perform "in-the-round."
The students surround the stage on all four sides, and
Bridgework brings their own sound system, microphones, and
stage. 2) They hire professional, adult actors. They are well-
trained, friendly, and very good with children. They involve up
to four students as reader-actors in each performance, and the
students rehearse with the Bridgeworks actors before the performance.

Imagination Theater
    1801 W. Byron, #2-S
    Chicago, IL 60613
    (773) 929-4100
    e-mail: info@imaginationtheater.org
    www.imaginationtheater.org

Imagination Theater (IT) is a touring, educational theater
company with programs on teasing, conflict resolution, personal body safety, and substance-abuse prevention. Professional
psychotherapists accompany each Imagination show to provide
post-show crisis counseling and referral and follow-up services.

OTHER RELATED PROGRAMS

Jigsaw Classroom
Created by Elloit Aronson, Professor Emeritus at the
University of California at Santa Cruz and the author of
Nobody Left to Hate: Teaching Compassion After Columbine

(New York: Henry Holt, 2000), the jigsaw classroom is a specific cooperative-learning technique with a three-decade track record of success. Just as in a jigsaw puzzle each piece is essential for the completion and full understanding of the final product, so in a classroom each student has an essential part. Because each student's part is essential, then each student is essential, and that is precisely what makes this strategy so effective. While the teaching method is not designed to combat bullying directly, many have found that is one of its results, since it encourages inclusion and cooperation.

Here is how it works: The students in a history class, for example, are divided into small groups of five or six students each. Suppose their task is to learn about World War II. In one jigsaw group, Sara is responsible for researching Hitler's rise to power in prewar Germany; another member of the group, Steven, is assigned to cover concentration camps; Pedro is assigned Britain's role in the war; Melody is to research the contribution of the Soviet Union; Tyrone will handle Japan's entry into the war; and Clara will read about the development of the atom bomb.

"Eventually each student will come back to her or his jigsaw group and will try to present a well-organized report to the group. The situation is specifically structured so that the only access any member has to the other five assignments is by listening closely to the report of the person reciting. Thus, if Tyrone doesn't like Pedro, or if he thinks Sara is a nerd and tunes her out or makes fun of her, he cannot possibly do well on the test that follows."

Advocates claim that it is not only a remarkably efficient way to learn the material, but the jigsaw process also encourages listening, engagement, and empathy by giving each member of the group an essential part to play in the academic activity.

Group members must work together as a team to accomplish a common goal; each person depends on all the others. No student can succeed completely unless everyone works well together as a team. This "cooperation by design" facilitates interaction among all students in the class, leading them to value each other as contributors to their common task.

Blueprints for Violence Prevention
　　Center for the Study and Prevention of Violence
　　Institute of Behavioral Science
　　University of Colorado at Boulder
　　900 28th Street, Suite 107
　　439 UCB
　　Boulder, CO 80309-0439
　　(303) 492-1032
　　Fax (303) 443-3297
　　Email: blueprint@colorado.edu

In 1996, the Center for the Study and Prevention of Violence (CSPV) at the University of Colorado at Boulder, designed and launched a national violence prevention initiative to identify and replicate violence prevention programs that are effective. The project, called Blueprints for Violence Prevention, has identified eleven prevention and intervention programs that meet a strict scientific standard of program effectiveness. Program effectiveness is based upon an initial review by CSPV and a final review and recommendation from a distinguished advisory board, comprised of seven experts in the field of violence prevention. The eleven model programs, called Blueprints, have been effective in reducing adolescent violent crime, aggression, delinquency, and substance abuse. Another nineteen programs have been identified as promising programs.

To date, more than five hundred programs have been reviewed, and the Center continues to look for programs that meet the selection criteria. The Blueprints Initiative is a comprehensive effort to provide communities with a set of effective programs and the technical assistance and monitoring necessary to plan for and develop effective violence intervention.

WEB SITES AND RESOURCE CENTERS

Bully B'ware Productions
1421 King Albert Avenue
Coquitlam, British Columbia
Canada V3J 1Y3
Telephone/Fax: (604) 936-8000
(888) 552-8559
e-mail: bully@direct.ca
www.bullybeware.com

This is a helpful Web site that collects articles and information on bullying and summarizes the key concepts behind understanding, preventing, and dealing with bullying in schools. In addition, Bully B'ware Productions has a book, video, and posters to help students, parents, teachers and administrators "Take Action Against Bullying." They also run workshops for school staff.

National School Safety Center
141 Duesenberg Drive
Suite 11
Westlake Village, CA 91362
(805) 373-9977
www.nssc1.org

The National School Safety Center was created by presidential directive in 1984 to meet the growing need for additional training and preparation in the area of school crime and violence prevention. Their programs and resources emphasize ways to rid schools of crime, violence, and drugs, and they also emphasize programs to improve student discipline, attendance, achievement, and school climate. NSSC provides technical assistance, legal and legislative aid, and publications and films. They conduct training programs and provide technical assistance for education and law enforcement practitioners, as well as for legislators and other key governmental policy shapers. In addition, NSSC serves as a clearinghouse for current information on school safety issues, maintaining a resource center with more than fifty thousand articles, publications, and films. Many articles are available on their Web site. They also sponsor The School Safety News Service and publish a journal, *School Safety Update*.

CBC, *The National*
  Box 14,000 Station A
  Toronto Ontario M5W 1E6
  Canada
  Phone: (416) 205-6384
  Fax: (416) 205-3482
  E-mail: edsales@toronto.cbc.ca

Canada's public broadcasting station, CBC, broadcast two specials on bullying in 2001 in their nightly news show *The National*. Both specials captured the attention of Canadian viewers and were widely watched and discussed. They offer a fair, well-rounded introduction to the topic of bullying and are available for purchase on their web page. In addition, many portions of the documentaries (four-to-eighteen-minute segments) can be seen online through streaming video, with corresponding articles and links to other sites on bullying. Overall, this is an excellent window into understanding bullying.

ERIC Digests
ERIC Digests are short reports (1,000–1,500 words) on topics of prime current interest in education. They are targeted specifically for teachers, administrators, policymakers, and other practitioners but are generally useful to the broad educational community. They are designed to provide an overview of information on a given topic, plus references to items providing more detailed information. They are funded by the U.S. Department of Education. Search for articles on bullying, peer mediation, and many other relevant topics. This is a very helpful resource for getting good professional information quickly and concisely.

Let's Talk About Bullying
Family Service Canada
383 Parkdale Avenue, Suite 404
Ottawa, Ontario, Canada, K1Y 4R4
(613) 722-9006 or (800) 668-7808
(800) 668-6868 (kids hotline)

A phone and Web hotline where kids can report bullying activity. The site is administered by Family Service Canada and promises anonymity.

PTA
As might be expected, the PTA Web site has a number of articles on bullying, sexual harassment, school violence, and many other topics.

National Education Association
A database with helpful articles on the subject of bullying.

BOOKS AND MANUALS

Best Friends, Worst Enemies: Understanding the Social Lives of Children
    Michael Thompson & Catherine O'Neill Grace with Lawrence Cohen
    Ballantine Books
    2001

Breaking Down the Wall of Anger: Interactive Games & Activities
    Ester Williams
    Youthlight, Inc.
    2000

Anger management curriculum for 5th to 8th grade.

Bullies and Victims: Helping Your Child through the Schoolyard Battlefield
    Suellen Fried and Paula Fried
    M. Evans
    1996

One of the best and most comprehensive treatments of bullying for a wide audience.

Bully Busters: A Teacher's manual for Helping Bullies, Victims, and Bystanders
    Dawn Newman, Arthur Horne, & Christi Bartolomucci
    Research Press
    2000

The Bully Prevention Handbook
    John H. Hoover and Ron Oliver
    National Education Service
    1997

A much used and admired guidebook.

Cliques: 8 Steps to Help Your Child Survive the Social Jungle
    Charlene C. Giannetti and Margaret Sagarese
    Broadway Books
    2001

The Gift of Fear: Survival Signals That Protect Us from Violence
    Gavin de Becker
    Little Brown & Co
    1997

How and When to Tell Your Kids About Sex
    Stanton L. Jones and Brenna B. Jones
    NavPress
    1993

Lost Boys: Why Our Sons Turn Violent and How We Can Save Them
    James Garbarino
    Anchor Books
    1999

Playground Politics: Understanding the Emotional Life of your School-Aged Child
    Stanley Greenspan
    Perseus
    1993

The 7 Habits of Highly Effective Teens: The Ultimate Teenage Success Guide
    Sean Covey
    Simon & Schuster
    1998

Sean Covey adapts his father's materials for high school students. Many educators have found his core habits to be a helpful framework for a character curriculum.

Stick Up for Yourself: Every Kid's Guide to Personal Power and Positive Self-Esteem
    Gershen Kaufman, Lev Raphael, and Pamela Espeland
    Free Spirit
    1999

Why Doesn't Anybody Like Me? A Guide to Raising Socially Confident Kids
    Hara Estroff Marano
    Quill
    1998

The Wounded Spirit Video Curriculum
    Frank Peretti
    The W Publishing Group
    2001

A complete curriculum for church youth groups based on Frank Peretti's book, *The Wounded Spirit*. The packet includes the video, complete materials for five group meetings, and reproducible handouts for kids to work on at home.

Appendix B
Myths and Facts about Bullying

Respect & Protect by Carol Remboldt; copyright © 1994 by Hazelden Foundation. Reprinted by permission of Hazelden Foundation, Center City, MN.

Myths	Facts
1. Bullying only occurs in big city schools and is often related to gangs.	1. Higher in rural areas/small towns.
2. Caused by large class size.	2. Size of class is of negligible importance.
3. Occurs on way to/from school.	3. The school or school grounds are where most bullying occurs.
4. Occurs chiefly among poor/disadvantaged students	4. Found in all socio-economic levels of students.
5. More pervasive in upper grades.	5. Most pervasive among older students in lower grades.
6. All bullies are anxious and insecure with poor self-esteem.	6. Some bullies have positive view of self with little anxiety.
7. Bullying is a result of poor grades or of failures at school.	7. Bullies are within the average range in both marks and competitiveness.
8. Bullies are only aggressive to peers and fellow students.	8. Bullies are often aggressive to adults, both parents and teachers.
9. Only boys are victims of bullying	9. Boys are exposed more to direct forms and open attack. Girls are exposed more to indirect acts.
10. Girls are usually bullied by girls.	10. Boys are the chief bullies with both boys and girls.
11. Bullies can change by treating them kindly or punishing them.	11. Bullies need consequences, restitution, activities for learning.
12. Peer mediation is effective with bullies.	12. Bullies can threaten or con their way out with peers.

Myths	Facts
13. Bullying behavior disappears with age.	13. Bullying behavior can last into adulthood if no intervention is made.
14. Bullies are unpopular kids.	14. Bullies have followers. Victims become shunned and isolated.
15. Bullying is more likely to be to kids who "look funny" or are "physically deviant or different" than others.	15. These conditions may evoke, but do not cause bullying.
16. Teachers can do nothing with bullies or victims.	16. Teachers can effectively help stop bullying by using a systematic approach.

Sources: Olweus, Dan. *Bullying at School: What We Know and What We Can Do*. Cambridge: Blackwell Publishers, 1993; Wheeler, Eugene, and S. Anthony Baron. *Violence in Our Schools, Hospitals and Public Places: A Prevention and Management Guide*. Ventura: Pathfinders Publishing of California, 1994.

Appendix C
Characteristics of Youth Who Have Caused School-Associated Violent Deaths

T he National School Safety Center offers the following checklist derived from tracking school-associated violent deaths in the United States from July 1992 to the present. After studying common characteristics of youngsters who have caused such deaths, NSSC has identified the following behaviors, which could indicate a youth's potential for harming him/herself or others.

Accounts of these tragic incidents repeatedly indicate that in most cases, a troubled youth has demonstrated or has talked to others about problems with bullying and feelings of isolation, anger, depression, and frustration. While there is no foolproof system for identifying potentially dangerous students who may harm themselves and/or others, this checklist provides a starting point.

These characteristics should serve to alert school administrators, teachers and support staff to address needs of troubled students through meetings with parents, provision of school counseling, guidance, and mentoring services, as well as referrals to appropriate community health/social services and law enforcement personnel. Further, such behavior should also provide an early warning signal that safe school plans and crisis prevention/intervention procedures must be in place to protect the health and safety of all school students and staff members so that schools remain safe havens for learning.

_____ Has a history of tantrums and uncontrollable angry outbursts.

_____ Characteristically resorts to name calling, cursing, or abusive language.

_____ Habitually makes violent threats when angry.

_____ Has previously brought a weapon to school.

_____ Has a background of serious disciplinary problems at school and in the community.

_____ Has a background of drug, alcohol, or other substance abuse or dependency.

_____ Is on the fringe of his/her peer group with few or no close friends.

_____ Is preoccupied with weapons, explosives, or other incendiary devices.

_____ Has previously been truant, suspended, or expelled from school.

_____ Displays cruelty to animals.

_____ Has little or no supervision and support from parents or a caring adult.

_____ Has witnessed or been a victim of abuse or neglect in the home.

_____ Has been bullied and/or bullies or intimidates peers or younger children.

_____ Tends to blame others for difficulties and problems s/he causes her/himself.

_____ Consistently prefers TV shows, movies, or music expressing violent themes and acts.

_____ Prefers reading materials dealing with violent themes, rituals, and abuse.

_____ Reflects anger, frustration, and the dark side of life in school essays or writing projects.

_____ Is involved with a gang or an antisocial group on the fringe of peer acceptance.

_____ Is often depressed and/or has significant mood swings.

_____ Has threatened or attempted suicide.

Developed by the National Safety Center © 1998
Dr. Ronald D. Stephens, Executive Director
141 Duesenberg Dr., Suite 11, Westlake Village, CA 91362
Phone (805) 373–9977; Fax (805) 373–9277

Appendix D
Things Children Should Know to Protect Themselves

Do your children know . . .

1. how to honor their feelings? If someone makes them uncomfortable, that's an important signal.
2. you (the parents) are strong enough to hear about any experience they've had, no matter how unpleasant?
3. it's okay to rebuff and defy adults to protect themselves?
4. it's okay to be assertive?
5. how to ask for assistance or help?
6. how to choose who to ask?
7. how to describe their peril?
8. it's okay to strike, even to injure, someone if they believe they are in danger, and that you'll support any action they take as a result of feeling uncomfortable or afraid?
9. it's okay to make noise, to scream, to yell, to run?

10. if someone ever tries to force them to go somewhere, what they scream should include, "This is not my father," because onlookers seeing a child scream or even struggle are likely to assume the adult is a parent?
11. if someone says, "Don't yell," the thing to do is yell; if someone says, "Don't tell" the thing to do is tell?
12. to fully resist ever going anywhere out of public view with someone they don't know, and particularly to resist going anywhere with someone who tries to persuade them?

From *Protecting the Gift*, by Gavin de Becker. Dial Press, 1999.

Appendix E
16 Sure Signs of Strong Self-Esteem

Your self esteem is strong when . . .

1. it doesn't depend on whether things always go right in your life.
2. you enjoy your successes because they make you feel proud inside, not because other people praise you.
3. you do good things for others without expecting anything in return.
4. you are not afraid to talk about your talents and abilities, but you don't exaggerate or brag.
5. you don't worry too much about failing or looking foolish.
6. you don't make excuses for your mistakes. You claim them and learn something useful from each one.
7. you're assertive—you say what you want and need—but not bossy.
8. you're mostly happy with yourself the way you are.
9. you don't need to put other people down to feel good about yourself.

10. you can do many things for yourself, but you ask for help when you need it.
11. you accept compliments, but you don't get a swelled head.
12. you listen to criticism, but you don't let it drag you down.
13. you don't get defensive when someone questions you.
14. you don't get angry when someone challenges you.
15. you care about achievement, but you don't push yourself too hard or try to be perfect.
16. you can laugh at yourself.

Endnotes

CHAPTER ONE

1. Hamad's story is public knowledge. In all cases of personal stories that are not public knowledge, however, the names and circumstances and other details have been changed to protect the privacy of those who shared their stories with the author.
2. Tonja R. Nansel, *Journal of the American Medical Association* (25 April 2001).
3. Study cited by Suellen Fried and Paula Fried, *Bullies and Victims* (N.Y.: M. Evans, 1996), xi.
4. For an excellent summary of current research on bullying, see Ron Banks, "Bullying in Schools," *ERIC Digest* (March 1997); www.ed.gov/databases/ERIC_Digests/ed407154.html. *ERIC Digest* is an online educational resource sponsored by the U.S. Department of Education, www.ed.gov/databases/ERIC_Digests. The study referred to is from Dan Olweus, *Bullying at School: What We Know and What We Can Do* (Cambridge, Mass.: Blackwell, 1993).
5. Banks, "Bullying in Schools."
6. Louise A. Dietzel, *Parenting with Respect and Peacefulness* (Lancaster, Pa.: Starburst, 1995), 104.
7. Ibid.
8. Ibid., 87.
9. Banks, "Bullying in Schools."
10. Fried and Fried, *Bullies and Victims*, 9–10.
11. Michael Thompson, Catherine O'Neill Grace, with Lawrence J. Cohen, *Best Friends, Worst Enemies: Understanding the Social Lives of Children* (N.Y.: Ballantine, 2001), 101.

12. Preliminary report from the National Task Force on Juvenile Sexual Offending, *Juvenile and Family Court Journal* 38, no. 2 (National Adolescent Perpetrator Network, 1988), 1–67.
13. Fried and Fried, *Bullies and Victims*, 67.
14. "Hostile Hallways," a report by the American Association of University Women, 1993.
15. Cited in Fried and Fried, *Bullies and Victims*, 61.
16. Dan Olweus, *Bullying at School* (Cambridge, Mass.: Blackwell, 1993).

CHAPTER 2

1. Banks, "Bullying in Schools."
2. G. M. Batsche and H. M. Knoff, "Bullies and Their Victims: Understanding a Pervasive Problem in the Schools," *School Psychology Review* 23, no. 2 (1994), 165–74. Dan Olweus, *Bullying at School* (Cambridge, Mass.: Blackwell, 1993).
3. National School Safety Center resource paper, "School Bullying and Victimization."
4. Ibid.
5. Ibid.
6. American Psychiatric Association, *Diagnostic and Statistical Manual of Mental Disorders*, 4th ed. (Washington, D.C., American Psychiatric Association, 1994), 645-50.
7. Barry E. McNamara and Francine McNamara, *Keys to Dealing with Bullies* (Hauppauge, N.Y.: Baron's, 1997), 4.
8. Ibid., 4–5.
9. Cited in Fried and Fried, *Bullies and Victims*, 91.
10. McNamara and McNamara, *Keys to Dealing with Bullies*, 5.
11. Banks, "Bullying in Schools."
12. Dietzel, *Parenting with Respect and Peacefulness*, 88.
13. K. A. Dodge and J. D. Coie, "Social Information Processing Factors in Reactive and Proactive Aggression in Children's Peer Groups," *Journal of Personality and Social Psychology* 53 (1987), 1146–58. Cited in Fried and Fried, *Bullies and Victims*, 87–88.
14. Banks, "Bullying in Schools."
15. McNamara and McNamara, *Keys to Dealing with Bullies*, 5.
16. National School Safety Center resource paper, "School Bullying and Victimization," 5.
17. Richard B. Goldbloom, "Parents' Primer on School Bullying," *Reader's Digest–Canada* (October 2001).

Endnotes

CHAPTER 3

1. Frank Peretti, *The Wounded Spirit* (Nashville: Word, 2000), 60–61.
2. Ibid., 130.
3. Richard B. Goldbloom, "Parents' Primer on School Bullying," *Reader's Digest–Canada* (October 2001).
4. Ron Banks, "Bullying in Schools," *ERIC Digest* (March 1997).
5. Suellen Fried and Paula Fried, *Bullies and Victims*, 96.
6. Ibid., 97.
7. McNamara and McNamara, *Keys to Dealing with Bullies*, 17–18.
8. Ibid., 2.
9. Banks, "Bullying in School."
10. McNamara and McNamara, *Keys to Dealing with Bullies*, 3.
11. Ibid., 9.
12. From a news release of the National Institutes of Health (24 April 2001).
13. Banks, "Bullying in Schools."
14. Reported in Banks, "Bullying in Schools."
15. Goldbloom, "Parents' Primer on School Bullying."

CHAPTER 4

1. McNamara and McNamara, *Keys to Dealing with Bullies*, 10.
2. Debra J. Pepler, LaMarsh Centre for Research on Violence and Conflict Resolution, York University.
3. Cited in Goldbloom, "Parents' Primer on School Bullying."
4. Jane Clifford, "Facing Down the Enemy," *San Diego Union Tribune* (14 April 2001).
5. Ibid.
6. Cited in Fried and Fried, *Bullies and Victims*, 60.
7. Stanton L. Jones and Brenna B. Jones, *How and When to Tell Your Kids About Sex* (Colorado Springs: NavPress, 1993), 164.
8. Ibid., 173.
9. Peretti, *The Wounded Spirit*, 125–26.
10. Ibid., 127.
11. Frank Peretti, The Wounded Spirit video curriculum (Nashville: W Publishing Group, 2001).
12. From "Tips and Strategies," Bully B'Ware Productions, www.bullybeware.com.
13. Ibid.
14. Fried and Fried, *Bullies and Victims*, 112.
15. Ibid.

16. Ibid.
17. Gavin de Becker, *The Gift of Fear: Survival Signals That Protect Us from Violence* (N.Y.: Little Brown, 1997), 26.
18. Ibid.
19. Charlene C. Giannetti and Margaret Sagarese, *Cliques: 8 Steps to Help Your Child Survive the Social Jungle* (N.Y.: Broadway Books, 2001), 110–14.
20. Cindi Seddon, "Tips and Strategies," Bully B'Ware Productions, www.bullybeware.com.
21. Ibid.
22. Fried and Fried, *Bullies and Victims*, 112.
23. Ibid.
24. Fried and Fried, *Bullies and Victims*, 112.
25. Jones and Jones, *How and When to Tell Your Kids About Sex*, 172–73.
26. Giannetti and Sagarese, *Cliques*, 137–41.
27. Fried and Fried, *Bullies and Victims*, 111–12.
28. Frank Peretti, The Wounded Spirit video curriculum.

CHAPTER 5
1. Barry E. McNamara and Francine McNamara, *Keys to Dealing with Bullies* (Hauppauge, N.Y.: Baron's, 1997), 8–9.
2. Goldbloom, "Parents' Primer on School Bullying."
3. Ibid.
4. McNamara and McNamara, *Keys to Dealing with Bullies*, 10.
5. Ibid., 11.
6. Clifford, "Facing Down the Enemy."
7. Ibid.

CHAPTER 6
1. Banks, "Bullying in Schools."
2. Clifford, "Facing Down the Enemy."

CHAPTER 7
1. David Keller Trevaskis, "Mediation in the Schools," *ERIC Digest* (December 1994).
2. Ibid.
3. Ibid.
4. Ibid.
5. Cited in Linda Starr, "Bullying Strategies That Work," *Educational World* (12 July 2000).

ENDNOTES

APPENDICES

1. Summarized by Marlies Sudermann, Peter G. Jaffe, and Elaine Schieck, "Bullying: Information for Parents and Teachers," London Family Court Clinic (1996).
2. See program directions at www.jigsaw.org.

Bibliography

Banks, Ron. "Bullying in Schools." *ERIC Digest* (March 1997).

Batsche, G. M., and H. M. Knoff. "Bullies and Their Victims: Understanding a Pervasive Problem in the Schools." *School Psychology Review 23*, no. 2 (1994): 165–74.

Bully B'Ware Productions. www.bullybeware.com.

Clifford, Jane. "Facing Down the Enemy." *The San Diego Union Tribune* (14 April 2001).

De Becker, Gavin. *The Gift of Fear: Survival Signals That Protect Us from Violence*. N.Y.: Little Brown, 1997.

Dietzel, Louise A. *Parenting with Respect and Peacefulness*. Lancaster, Pa: Starburst, 1995.

Dodge, K. A., and J. D. Coie. "Social Information Processing Factors in Reactive and Proactive Aggression in Children's Peer Groups." *Journal of Personality and Social Psychology 53* (1987): 1146–58.

Fried, Suellen, and Paula Fried. *Bullies and Victims*. N.Y.: M. Evans, 1996.

Giannetti, Charlene C., and Margaret Sagarese. *Cliques: 8 Steps to Help Your Child Survive the Social Jungle*. N.Y.: Broadway Books, 2001.

Goldbloom, Richard. "Parents' Primer on School Bullying." *Readers Digest*-Canada (October 2001).

Jones, Stanton L., and Brenna B. Jones. *How and When to Tell Your Kids About Sex*. Colorado Springs: NavPress, 1993.

McNamara, Barry E., and Francine McNamara. *Keys to Dealing with Bullies*. Hauppauge, N.Y.: Baron's, 1997.

Olweus, Dan. Bullying at School. Cambridge, Mass.: Blackwell, 1993.

Peretti, Frank. *The Wounded Spirit*. Nashville: Word, 2000.

—-. The Wounded Spirit video curriculum. Nashville: The W Publishing Group, 2001.

Schrumpf, Fred. *Peer Mediation: Conflict Resolution in Schools: Program Guide*. Champaign, Ill.: Research Press, 1997.

Schrumpf, Fred, D. Crawford, and H. Usadel. *Peer Mediation: Conflict Resolution in Schools*. Champaign, Ill.: Research Press, 1997.

Starr, Linda. "Bullying Strategies That Work." *Educational World* (12 July 2000).

Sudermann, Marlies, Peter G. Jaffe, and Elaine Schieck. "Bullying: Information for Parents and Teachers." London Family Court Clinic (1996).

Trevaskis, David Keller. "Mediation in the Schools," *ERIC Digest* (December 1994).

About the Author

Karen Maudlin, Psy.D., is the parenting expert for *Christian Parenting Today* (a magazine of Christianity Today International) and a psychologist in private practice in the Chicago area. A graduate of Miami University, Wheaton College, and the Chicago School of Professional Psychology, Dr. Maudlin works with children, adolescents, and their families. She is an expert in working with children of divorce and supervises doctoral psychology students in training at a local free clinic. As a part of her work with children, she coordinates with area schools and offers programs for parents and administrators. Karen is also an Adjunct Clinical Faculty for the doctoral program in psychology at Wheaton College. She has written numerous articles pertaining to family life, including a family devotional series. She and her husband, Michael, have two children.